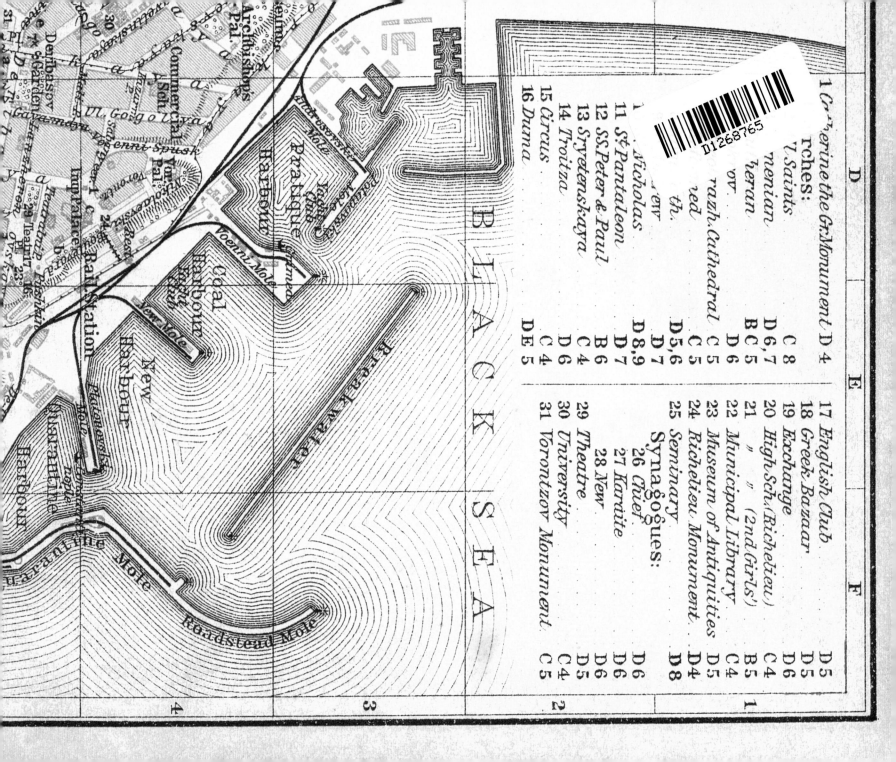

1 Catherine the Gr. Monument ... D 4
Churches:
... Saints ... C 8
... menian ... D 6,7
... heran ... B C 5
...ov ... D 6
...razh. Cathedral ... C 5
...red ... C 5
...th. ... D 5,6

...ew ... D 7
1. Nicholas ... D 8,9
11 St Pantaleon ... D 7
12 SS. Peter & Paul ... B 6
13 Sryetenskaya ... C 4
14 Troitza ... D 6
15 Circus ... C 4
16 Duma ... D E 5

17 English Club ... D 5
18 Greek Bazaar ... D 5
19 Exchange ... D 6
20 High Sch. (Richelieu) ... C 4
21 „ „ (2nd Girls') ... B 5
22 Municipal Library ... C 4
23 Museum of Antiquities ... D 5
24 Richelieu Monument ... D 4
25 Seminary ... D 8
Synagogues:
26 Chief ... D 6
27 Karaite ... D 6
28 New ... D 6
29 Theatre ... D 5
30 University ... C 4
31 Vorontzov Monument ... C 5

BLACK SEA

Breakwater
New Harbour
Coal Harbour
Quarantine Harbour
Raidstead Mole
Quarantine Mole
Yacht Club
Pratique Harbour

Odessa Memories

Left: An advertisement for the confectionery factory of the Italian entrepreneur N. M. Ambatiello, 1897. *Below:* Odessa, early 1900s.

Odessa, early 1900s.

Clockwise from left: Promenade and view of the harbor from the Gigantskaya steps (Potemkin Steps). Colored postcard, early 1910s; Advertisement for cigarettes from I. Asvadurov and Sons; Church of St. Panteleimon, 1910s. Postcard, 1916. *Pages vi–xvi*: Streetscapes and seascapes from the early 1900s. Postcards.

Лиманно-свѣто-лѣчебное заведеніе
Врача В. Д. Глѣбовой на Хаджи-
бейскомъ Лиманѣ. Г. Одесса.
Уголокъ для отдыха.

Одесса. Дѣтскій садъ внизу бульвара.

ОДЕССА ВЪ СНѢГУ   ДЕРИБАСОВСКАЯ УЛИЦА

Одесса · Буфетъ при курзалѣ Андріевскаго лимана
Odessa · Buffet auprès de la Salle du Liman Andreyevski

Одесса. Большой фонтанъ — 16ая станцiя.
Odessa. Grande Fontaine — 16me station.

Одесса. Подъемная машина.

Одесса – Odessa Видъ на Николаевскiй Бульваръ съ террасы Городской думы
Boulevard de Nicolas vu de la terrasse de l'hôtel de ville

Одесса

Odessa
Fronton principal de l'Etablissement
manois dans de Liman Andreyevski

Odessa. Memories

Edited by **Nicolas V. Iljine**

Essay by **Patricia Herlihy**

Contributions by
**Bel Kaufman,
Oleg Gubar and
Alexander Rozenboim**

A Samuel and Althea Stroum Book

University of Washington Press
Seattle & London

This book is published with the assistance of a grant from the Stroum Book
Fund, established through the generosity of Samuel and Althea Stroum.

University of Washington Press
P.O. Box 5096
Seattle, WA 98145
www.washington.edu/uwpress

The paper used in this publication meets the minimum
requirements of American National Standard for Information Sciences—Permanence of Paper for Printed Library
Materials, ANSI Z39.48–1984.

Library of Congress Cataloging-in-Publication Data

Odessa memories / edited by Nicolas V. Iljine ; essay
by Patricia Herlihy ; contributions by Bel Kaufman,
Oleg Gubar and Alexander Rozenboim.
p. cm.
"A Samuel and Althea Stroum book."
ISBN 0-295-98345-0 (cloth : alk. paper)
1. Odesa (Ukraine)—History—19th century. 2. Odesa
(Ukraine)—Intellectual life—19th century. I. Iljine,
Nicolas V.

DK508.95.O33O327   2004
947.7'2083'0922—dc21   2003055242

Title-page spread, pp. xviii–xix: Preobrazhenskaya Street viewed
from Deribasovskaya Street. Color postcard (detail), early 1910s.
Opposite: An ad of the Odessa Society of Artificial Mineral Waters
(1829) one of the society's founders was the Swiss chemist and
physician Enno.

Contents

Nadezhda Panteleimonovna Ksida received first prize for her costume as Lotto at a ball organized by the Odessa Chapter of the Imperial Russian Technical Society, 8 December 1912.

Ilya Pheophilaktovich Pavlov (first from right), a shipping broker, liked to play whist with friends in the English Club, over a bottle of good wine or beer. Photograph, early twentieth century.

Одесса.   Русскій хоръ.   Odessa.

Simple "Russian" or "Gypsy" choirs like this amused
Odessa gentlemen in restaurants and taverns. Postcard.
early twentieth-century.

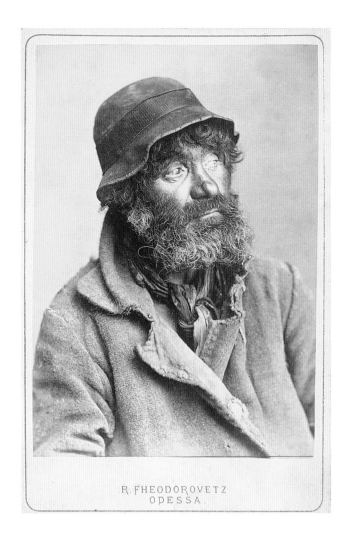

R. FHEODOROVETZ
ODESSA.

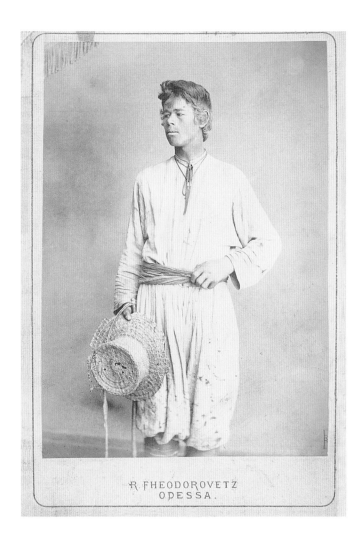

R. FHEODOROVETZ
ODESSA.

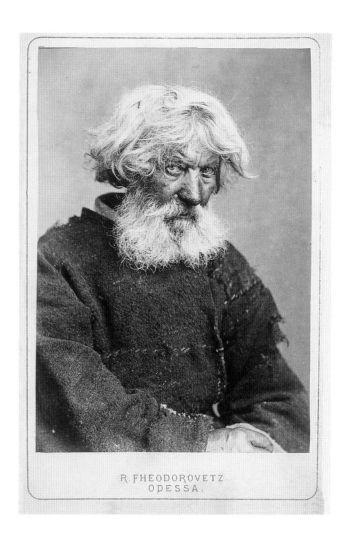

Above and opposite: Portraits taken by Odessa photographer
Rudolf Feodorovets, 1860s–1870s.

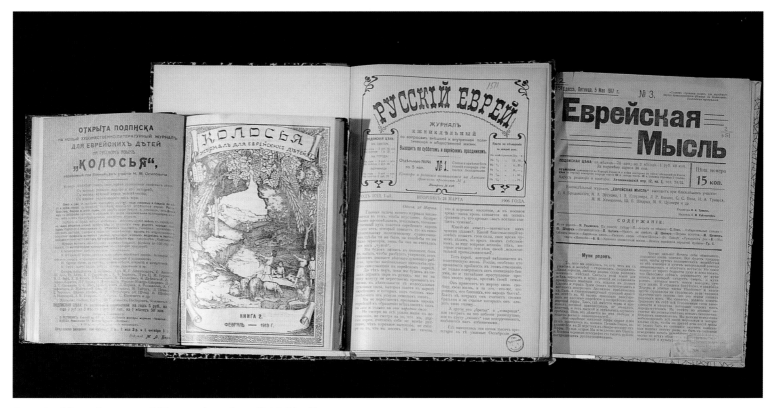

Opposite: Musical scores and librettos (mostly in Yiddish). *Above:* Jewish periodicals *Kolosiya* (Ears of Wheat), *Russkii Evrei* (Russian Jew), and *Evreiskaya Mysl'* (Jewish Thought), early twentieth century.

Russian Orthodox Cathedral of the Transfiguration, completed in 1848. *Opposite:* Construction of one of the port's moorings. Photograph, late 1860s–early 1870s.

Preface

Nicolas V. Iljine

The first recollection I have of Odessa is my parents telling me that my godfather, Nikolai Poltoratzky, had left Paris in the late 1940s in order to go back to Odessa to assist his ailing elderly mother, certainly a courageous step in those Stalinist times. Unfortunately, since I was five years old then, I don't remember him, but many people told me that he was a highly respected teacher at the Russian Orthodox seminary in Odessa. The next memory—one I share with many—is the dramatic scene on the famous steps in Eisenstein's film *The Battleship Potemkin*.

This book started as a collection of prerevolutionary postcards of Odessa. My fascination with life in what a popular song calls the "pearl by the sea" grew as I talked with historians, archivists, artists, and musicians about the city and its role in the development of Russian and world culture. As I sought out other images— of Jewish periodicals, advertisements, and circus posters—from museums and libraries, I found that I had a book on my hands.

Left and above (detail): Scene from *The Battleship Potemkin*, 1925, directed by Sergei Eisenstein. Courtesy of Naum Kleiman, Moscow Film Museum.

Odessa had an impact on more than just the people who were lucky enough to live there. In Parisian Russian émigré circles, Odessa was a mythical name representing the joyous, liberal, and tolerant culture of the Black Sea resort and bustling port city. As a child I heard recordings of Odessa songs by Vertinsky, Leschenko, Morfessi, Kozin, Utesov, and Bernes. In 1969 the Bee Gees brought out an album called *Odessa*. Russia's most famous bard, Vladimir Vysotsky, had a song "Moskva-Odessa." Today these melodies are still popular in Russia and of course in New York's Brighton Beach, which rightfully earned its name "Little Odessa."

Many famous writers and musicians came from Odessa. Isaac Babel's stories from Odessa were the delight of readers for decades. One of the greatest legends of the city is Sholom Aleichem, whose granddaughter, American writer Bel Kaufman, kindly contributed to this book. Kuprin's "Gambrinus" has vivid scenes set in old Odessa; Bagritsky, Katayev, Olesha, Il'f and Petrov, and Sasha Chernyi, just to name a few, came from the city. Pushkin was exiled there for several years, and Gogol, Bunin, and Gorki visited Odessa.

The Stolyarsky Music School trained world-class musicians like David Oistrakh and Emil Gilels. Chalyapin and Caruso sang at the Odessa Opera House and Anna Pavlova and Isadora Duncan danced there.

Artists loved Odessa, and Kandinsky, Exter, Leonid Pasternak (father of Boris), Aivazovsky, Larionov, Redko, and Tyshler spent time working there.

Ardent Zionists and Jewish intellectual leaders whose names adorn the streets of Tel Aviv, like Jabotinsky, Ditzengof, Byalik, Dubnov, and Pinsker, were natives of Odessa. Many of my American friends have grandparents who came from there. Captain Mike Burke always wanted to visit his grandmother's birthplace in Odessa. During the installation of his monumental Cor-Ten steel sculptural ensemble at the Guggenheim in Bilbao, Richard Serra told me that his family's origins were in Odessa.

Like no other city in the world, this one was a mix of Russian and Jewish culture, intermingling peacefully during most of its history. Yet, pogroms kindled by jealousy, trading competition, and later by the chauvinism prevalent in other parts of Russia swept through Odessa in 1821, 1871, 1905, and at other times. Odessa was a cosmopolitan, multinational, Mediterranean-style city unlike any other in the Russian Empire. Its elegance came from a strong cultural life in theaters and cafés, its beauty from the eclectic architecture in a stunning natural setting, its tourism from the fashionable seaside spas, and its vitality from strong commerce and trade. Even a first-time visitor is overcome with an inexplicable sense of nostalgia when strolling through the city's broad avenues, past beautiful buildings and monuments from the olden days.

I intended the book's title to remind the reader of the vibrant, effervescent life of this city in the period between the mid-1800s and the Russian Revolution of 1917, since these times were also documented in photographs. As ever, Odessites' renowned sense of humor helps them

and visitors overcome the sadness they feel when comparing the city's past glory and fading beauty with its more sorrowful fate today in economically troubled Ukraine.

ACKNOWLEDGMENTS

In compiling this book, my thanks go to Oleg Gubar and Alexander Rozenboim, authors of the commentary on the illustrations, whom I met in Odessa several years back. Professor Patricia Herlihy of Brown University, preeminent historian of Odessa in the West, contributed an essay that provides thehistorical background. In Odessa I received many suggestions and helpful guidance from Evgeniy Golubovsky, editor of *Worldwide Odessa News*; Feliks Kokhrikht, ardent supporter of the arts and editor of the monthly journal *Odessa*, and his wife, Tania Verbitskaya, who teaches at Odessa University; Elena Karakina and Anna Poltoratskaya at the charming little Literature Museum; Mikhail Poizner, who has a remarkable photographic collection; Natalya Polishuk and Natalya Yakovenko

Sergei Eisenstein with Isaac Babel during the filming of *Bezhin Meadow*, 1936. The film was destroyed in 1937 by order of Stalin for "formalism" and "mysticism." Courtesy of Naum Kleiman, Moscow Film Museum.

of the Fine Arts Museum; the artist Alexander Roitburd; and Georgi Issaev, Ivan Cherevatenko, and Sergei Kalmykov, local photographers who gave me valuable input. Thanks to Hans Hisch, Lufthansa's man in Odessa, for his logistical help.

Special thanks go to Yigal Kotler, Director of the Moldova branch of the American Jewish Joint Distribution Committee and author of a book on Jewish Odessa, whom I visited in Kishinev and who introduced me to the authors in Odessa.

This book would not have been possible without the support of Elena Barkhatova, head of the Prints Department at the National Library of Russia in St. Petersburg, who helped me in selecting many a photograph from the rich archives under her supervision.

I am grateful to Steven J. Zipperstein, Professor of Jewish Culture and History at Stanford University, author of the standard work on the cultural history of the Jews in Odessa, for generously sharing valuable information and introducing me to Yigal Kotler.

The help of others is also gratefully acknowledged. In Berlin that includes Tina Bauermeister, cultural entrepreneur between Russia and Germany; Haralampi Oroshakoff, artist and writer; and Alexander Fedorovskyi, enlightened businessman.

In New York, I was helped by Antonina W. Bouis, who acted as translator and agent for the book and who is a multifaceted cultural ambassador between Russia and the United States; Mila Los, who prints money, finds sponsors, and is always smiling; Thomas Krens, Director of the Solomon R. Guggenheim Foundation, whose support and patience allowed me to spend time on the research for this book; David E. Fishman of the Jewish Theological Seminary of America; and Zachary Baker and Krysia Fisher of YIVO Institute for Jewish Research in New York.

In Moscow, Pavel Khoroshilov, Deputy Minister of Culture, a trained art historian and Germanophile, kindly lent me several portraits from his photographic collection; and Mikhail Shydkoi, Minister of Culture, television star, and teacher of theater history introduced me to Oscar Feltsman, the talented and popular composer who was recently honored as Odessite of the Year and is currently creating a Russian-Jewish musical with the action—naturally—starting in Odessa. I am also grateful to Marina Loshak, Odessa-born gallery director and wife of Victor, Ambassador of Odessa in Moscow, and to Vitaly Rudchenko, the gifted photographer of ancient Russian churches from whom I received my first postcards of prerevolutionary Odessa.

My thanks also to Prince Vladimir Dolgorukyi, in Komarno (Slovakia), for providing several old photographs; Ohad Zmora, a friend and retired but hyperactive publisher from Nir Zvi, Israel; Alexander Kantsedikas, art historian from Caesarea with a never-ending enthusiasm for Russian-Jewish themes; Chucky Zaroni, one of Israel's foremost public relations experts; Walter Koschmal, professor at Erlangen University, and Peter Hilkes, of Osteuropa Institut, Munich, for many a helpful hint; as well as to Zhenya Rozinskiy, San Francisco based creator of an Odessa website.

Most important, I thank my wife, Christa, whose endless patience and encouragement finally led to the realization of this project.

Opposite: Mikhail Larionov, *Women Bathing at Sunset*, Odessa, 1903–4. Oil on canvas, 46 x 54.6 cm.

Одесса.   Судебныя Установленія.

Одесса. — Портъ и таможня.
Odessa. — Port et douane.

Одесса. Университетъ. Физико-химическій отдѣлъ.
Odessa. L'université. La section physico-chimique.

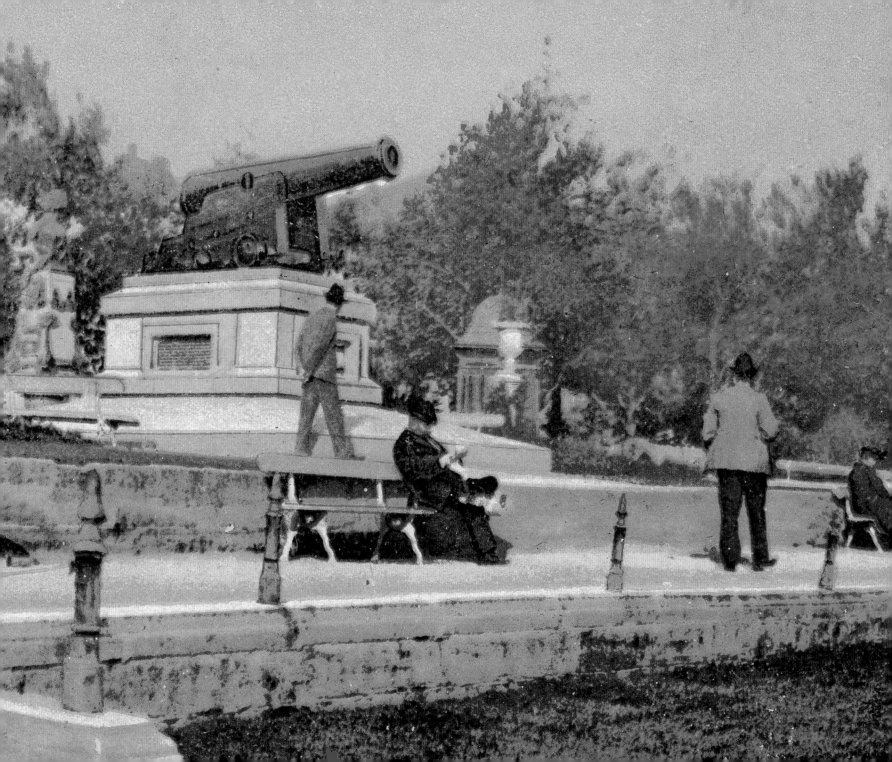

Одесская Выставка
Odessaer Ausstellung

Общи видъ Выставки
Total-Ansicht

Одесса. Почта.
Odessa. La poste.

Одесса. Биржевая площадь.

My Odessa

Bel Kaufman

In this panoramic book spanning many decades of old Odessa, this foreword is but one small girl's view of one small segment of the city's rich and colorful history. Its rare illustrations and photographs portray Odessa as it was before the Revolution of 1917; I have superimposed upon its vast historic map my own childhood memories of those turbulent days.

Odessa—"the golden city, the jewel on the sea"—the very name conjures up the sights, smells, tastes, and sounds of my childhood. The Odessa I knew was a city of poets and sailors, merchants and musicians, Jewish intellectuals and exotic strangers from beyond the Black Sea, like the two Chinese women I once saw walking on small stumps instead of shoes, or the Mandarin whose long, curling nails rested on a red pillow. I remember the wide boulevards, the chestnut trees, the steps leading to the sea. In summer—large yellow sunflowers on our dacha on Bolshoi Fontan; in winter—high snow banks, the sound of sleigh bells, and later, during the revolution, the sound of gunshots outside our window.

Left and above (detail): Bel Kaufman with her parents, Odessa, 1916.

I leap over eighty-five years to my early childhood. My father had studied medicine in Berlin, where I was born in 1911, and on our return to Odessa practiced it in our two-story house on Rishelyevskaya Street, no. 57. I remember our large black iron gate, too heavy for me to push. I remember it well because Vasska, the janitor's boy, once crushed my fingers in it. Behind the gate was a courtyard, and upstairs a balcony with the scent of acacias from the tree above it.

Childhood is a private place, crowded with first impressions and strong feelings. I remember jumping up and down in my crib, screaming with wordless joy when I saw my father, who had been away at "the front" in the war, towering above me in his splendid uniform.

My memories are not consecutive, but flashes of scenes and sensations. I remember my first taste of ice cream in a café on Deribasovskaya Street and my discovery of a delicious candy called Rakovye sheiki (Lobsters' necks). And of course there were the popular *semechki*, roasted sunflower seeds sold in large baskets on street corners. I would lift my apron for the saleswoman to pour a cupful into it and walk down the street practicing a newly learned skill: placing the *semechka* at a special angle against my two front teeth and clicking smartly twice, so that the kernel popped right into my mouth.

I remember the taste of chocolate during our famine, in the Hoover Package of food my grandmother sent us from America. We nibbled on it for days, like mice. My mother declared it to be far better than any chocolate she had had in Switzerland. It wasn't until we were in New York that we learned it was not for eating. It was cooking chocolate.

I remember my pride in my first published poem, a four-line paean to spring printed in a children's magazine, *Kolokol'chiki*, signed Belochka Koifman, 7 years. And my envy of the little girl in the park with the exotic name *Sylvia*, who wore a real wristwatch. How I wished I had her name, her watch! And how I longed to grow up to be like the older schoolgirls in their neat uniforms of brown dresses and black aprons, with the status book bags on their backs.

Papa Sholom Aleichem played an important role in my early childhood. We called him "Papa"; he was too youthful and full of fun to be a grandfather. He lived in New York during his last days, and he used to write me letters: TO ODESSA FROM AMERICA, FOR BELOCHKA. They have been preserved, and I have them before me now. In one, dated August 15, 1915, he writes in his minuscule Russian script:

> I am writing you that you have a war, we don't. And that you have a sea called the Black Sea and we have a sea called Atlantic Ocean. And I am writing also that I love you very very much and that I hope to see you and your mama and papa Michael, who will soon be a doctor. I am not a doctor, I am a writer.

> I am writing you this letter for you to grow up and learn to write me letters. And in order to grow up, it is necessary to drink milk, eat soup and vegetables and fewer candies. Regards to your dolls. Your Papa Sholom Aleichem.

I did grow up. I did learn to write—but not in time. In May 1916, a telegram arrived from New York with only three words in English: PAPA VERY SICK. It was understood what they meant.

Most vivid are my memories of the turbulent days of the Revolution of 1917—the chaos and confusion of the rapid changes of "temporary governments" occupying Odessa: *Bolsheviki, Mensheviki, Reds, Whites, Kerensky.* . . . The words were meaningless to me. Only one word, repeated in frightened whispers by the adults around me filled me with anxiety: *Cheka.* It was something that could take away my parents. Some names were fun, like the popular rhyming chant about the manufacturers of tea and sugar: *"Tea—Visotsky's; Sugar—Brodsky's; Russia—Trotsky's."*

We lived in peril, since we were the enemy *boorjoys* (bourgeois), with our own house and servants and possessions. I remember the Day of Peaceful Uprising. It was far from peaceful; it was a sort of Russian mini-pogrom. Soldiers burst into our house, among others, breaking things, taking things, shouting, and shooting. A man who had apparently tried to escape from the street into our courtyard was shot and killed. I was forbidden to come to the window, but of course I peeked. He lay there for several days in a grotesque frozen posture, his arm raised stiffly as if in a grim salute. The first day his shoes were gone, the next his jacket, then his pants. After a while, he was no longer there.

I remember standing in line for our ration of green bread made from the dried shells of peas, and I remember the taste of hunger.

Although we were not proletarians, I was sent off for a short time to a camp for the Children of the Proletariat because there, once in a while, the children were given a small piece of meat. I watched those children pull the meat apart into thin strings, to make it last. I did the same. One day my father brought me a precious gift: half of an orange. I hid it carefully under the pillow of my cot—but another child stole it. I can still recall my sense of outrage.

When I was nine my baby brother was born. One day I was wheeling him in his carriage on the street in front of our house when two young "new women" in leather jackets lifted him out of the carriage, thrust him into my skinny arms, said: "We have babies, too," and wheeled the carriage away. I remember going upstairs, my tears falling on the baby's blanket. "They have babies, too," I explained to my mother.

In between volleys of gunfire, during what we called the "calm days," our life in Odessa went on as normal. We had our Friday night *vecherinkas*—evenings when friends, Jewish writers and artists, came to visit. The poet Chaim-Nachman Byalik, and Ravnitsky, and Ben Ami, and a man by the name of Elman with his little son, Mischa, a violin prodigy. There were long grown-up discussions around the table about poetry and the price of firewood, and much laughter.

I recently came across an old diary of my mother's, in which she mentions a writer, an admirer of Sholom Aleichem, who had come unexpectedly.

> Of course, it was necessary to serve tea. Yet one could not serve tea without sugar. Since our small ration of sugar had to last a whole month, I placed the sugar bowl unobtrusively behind a vase on the table and began a lively flirtation with him in the hope that he wouldn't find it. He found it.

Everyone in our family wrote. While momentous political events were shaping history in Odessa, I was busy writing a drama—a play with a cast of many characters whom I described in the Dramatis Personae in minute detail: the color of their hair and eyes and socks, their coats and hats and hobbies. I wrote in a lined *tetradka*, notebook, with a pencil which, when wet with the tip of the tongue, wrote purple, and by the time I was about to start Act One, Scene One, there was no room left for the play itself. I still have that faded *tetradka*.

Whenever possible, my mother would drag us to a photographer. I hated those expeditions; it meant getting dressed up and holding my breath without moving for a long time. In one photograph, I am sitting between my two big dolls; they are dressed in clothes exactly like mine. In another, my father, mother, and I are posing in "native costumes"—Russian Cossack's hats and coats (p. xlviii).

Once a week a Hebrew teacher came to give me lessons. I can recall only one sentence, which I never found useful: "Anee hafeizo soos"—I want a horse.

What I liked best was reciting the poems of Pushkin, who at one time also lived in Odessa, and listening to Russian and Yiddish songs on the gramophone and hearing glowing stories about New York, where we would one day emigrate.

That day was inevitable. Several of my father's colleagues, *boorjoys* like us, were jailed or shot trying to cross the border. But Sholom Aleichem, posthumously, saved us. Even in the worst of times in Russia, he was translated, published, read widely, and cherished. We went to Moscow, where my mother managed to see Lunacharsky, the Minister of Culture. As Sholom Aleichem's daughter, she requested permission to go with her husband, daughter, and small son to visit her widowed mother in New York. Permission was granted, and we left in style, legally and safely.

Sholem Aleichem with his eighteen-month-old granddaughter
Bel Kaufman, Geneva, 1912.

BERLIN   3 YR

Bel Kaufman and her two dolls, which were featured in a poem by the
Yiddish poet Chaim-Nachman Byalik.

I did not return for forty-five years. In 1968, while in Moscow as guest of the Soviet Writers' Union, I arranged to make a brief visit to my Odessa. A woman was assigned to accompany me as guide or escort. We set out at once for my old home on Rishelyevskaya, no. 57. The street was now called Lenin Street and no. 57, we were told, was about to be razed, like all the rest of the dilapidated houses on the block. I did not recognize our house. Where was the large iron gate? A small rusty gate swung half off its hinges. The courtyard (where the dead man had been) was a muddy garbage dump. There was no acacia tree. We tried to enter, but a woman at the window screamed at us to go away.

I had come home a stranger. It was like meeting a distant, long-lost relative, and trying to make an emotional contact. The streets looked drab, the people glum and suspicious of an American.

I had occasional flashes of recognition. While my companion and I were walking on Deribasovskaya Street, we passed a large sigh: PASSAGE. A name suddenly swam into my mind. "Was this ever called Galantereinyi Passage?" I asked. It was, and I remembered my panic when I was lost, separated from my mother, who was in one of the stores shopping.

And here was the corner with the red balloons. It *was* the corner, but there were no red balloons.

The next day I managed to go out alone. I was walking down the wide steps leading to the pier (the famous Potemkin Steps). In one hand I held my pocketbook; my free arm kept unaccountably lifting itself up. I was puzzled, until I realized that as a child I could not navigate those steps without holding on to an adult's hand. My arm remembered what I did not.

To hear Russian spoken everywhere was thrilling, and even the *semechki* were still here; I hadn't lost the knack of popping the seeds. I wanted to revisit the beach on the Black Sea. What I found were sharp stones and blaring public address announcements and directions, as well as loud, ceaseless, unbidden music. "Why such loud music all the time?" I asked. "So that people wouldn't get depressed," was the answer.

Odessa was much livelier when I was there again thirty years later, in June 1998. This time I came as a VIP, a best-selling author, invited by the Jewish religious community to attend the unveiling of a plaque on 28 Kanatnaya Street, honoring my grandfather. It read, in Yiddish and Ukrainian:

IN THIS HOUSE FROM 1891 TO 1893 LIVED AND WORKED THE GREAT JEWISH
WRITER SHOLOM ALEICHEM (SHOLOM NAUMOVICH RABINOVICH) 1859–1916

A huge crowd, it seemed all who were left of the old Odessa Jewry, had gathered on Kanatnaya Street, thrusting questions, mikes, television cameras, Yiddish books, and letters at me, reading poems dedicated to my grandfather, giving speeches on the contribution of Jewish culture to Odessa, and expressing what my visit meant to them. They poured out their love for Sholom Aleichem, and it spilled over on me.

To my surprise, most had read my book, *Up the Down Staircase*, in Ukrainian translation, and many Ukrainian non-Jews were familiar with Sholom Aleichem.

Odessa was no longer a Soviet city; it was Ukrainian. The street on which I had once lived was no longer Lenin Street. It was once again Rishelyevskaya. I had no wish to see it. But I noted sadly that the former Sholom Aleichem Street was now called Myasoyedovskaya (Meat-eating). This was a busy city, bustling with people and cars, but on Primorskaya, the lovely boulevard abutting the sea, people were strolling slowly, families with children, some arm-in-arm or sitting on benches watching the sea.

Deribasovskaya was now quite Americanized: stands with Cokes, signs in English, sounds of jazz and rock. Strangers ran up to me with: "You're the granddaughter!"— recognizing me from television and newspapers. I bought an ice cream sandwich and walked licking it like a teenager.

Since Russian is my language, I was able to address many different audiences; the response of old-timers was overwhelming. In a Jewish old age home, Gimel Hessed, I was greeted with a special program on Sholom Aleichem and presented with a worn copy of the 1918 magazine *Kolokol'chiki*, in which my poem was circled in red.

I went to the still-noble Opera House, shamefully shabby inside, to hear an indifferent *Faust*. I visited the huge market, rich with aisles of vegetables and festoons of sausages. I walked on broken sidewalks, past half-remembered buildings, looking for my childhood. It wasn't there.

—March 2003

Odessa Memories

Одесса. — Подъемная Машина.
Odessa. — La funiculaire.

Odessa Memories

Patricia Herlihy

Odessa as a new town, as a boomtown, as a frontier city, attracted the best and the worst of Russian society. People with daring, entrepreneurial skills, and high hopes for freedom flocked there to find an El Dorado, or as the Yiddish saying promised, "to live like God in Odessa."[1] Others were already fugitives from the law, saw the commercial entrepôt as a potential for criminal activity, and sought their fortunes dishonestly. While many considered Odessites amoral as well as apolitical, most conceded that there were also many creative spirits in literature and the arts, sincere patriots, zealous reformers, good mothers and fathers. As Jabotinsky wrote, "Odessa was one of those few cities which created their own type of people."[2] Just as the city presents physical contrasts—the flatness of the steppes and the steepness of the bluffs, land and sea, sun and fog—Odessa's history presents light and dark passages.

Left and above (detail): Omnibus/funicular. Postcard, early 1900s.

Nature and history have conspired to create a singular, enchanting city by the sea—Odessa. The very name with its soft frame of vowels, its whispering sibilants, vaguely Greek, or perhaps Italian in origin, definitely not Slavic, is only the first of the city's many mysteries. Legends, not documents, say that the empress founder, Catherine II, gave a verbal order to name the city for the Greek epic hero Odysseus, but to render the word in the feminine gender. There are also tales that there had once been a Greek colony by that name in the vicinity, so that this was to be the second Odessa. The ancient Greek colony of Odessa, however, had been located in Bulgaria, many miles away.[3]

Odessa, easily pronounced by all tongues, was a kind of Esperanto city, or more accurately a Tower of Babel, reflecting the dozens of ethnic groups who carved out space within its capacious embrace, each speaking its own language, with Italian becoming the first lingua franca of the seaport. Only later did the Russian language predominate, but still twenty or more languages could be heard on the city's streets. An evocative place, Odessa has elicited stories, journals, histories, paintings, photographs, films, poetry, jokes, and songs across its two-hundred-year history from the famous and unknown to commemorate and even celebrate their experiences there.

Mysterious, magical, and majestic sitting on a high bluff overlooking the Black Sea, Odessa was also the scene of abject poverty, brutality, and violence. A popular Jewish song, "Odessa Mama," bespeaks the affection of the city's residents, but mothers can be cruel as well as kind. The unique mix of peoples in Odessa served as a matrix for creating wealth and art, but it was also a volatile mixture that sporadically erupted in dreadful pogroms and revolutions, as its darker pages of history record.

The city's very genesis was in violence, the forcible taking of the Turkish site by the Russian military in September 1789. And from the start, foreigners formed part of the city's history. Don Joseph de Ribas, a soldier of fortune born in Naples of Spanish

and Irish stock and one of the many adventurers in Catherine II's service, stormed the fortress and helped to secure it in September 1789. The Turks conceded the territory to Russia in 1792 by the Treaty of Jassy, where De Ribas was one of the three negotiators for Russia. Two years later began the transformation of the Turkish fort, Eni-Dunya (New World), on the site of the former village Khadzhibei, into Odessa.

Another foreigner, the Dutchman Francis De Wollant, or De Voland, as he was later called, was charged with building the new Russian fort. Having entered Catherine's service in 1787 from The Hague, he served in both the Russian Imperial army and navy, and was promoted to lieutenant-colonel engineer in 1791. The following year he was entrusted with the building of Odessa's port, stores, temporary quarantine buildings, and barracks. He is the first known resident of Odessa to leave his memoirs, which were not discovered until 1997.[4] Together with De Ribas, he drew up a plan for the city, and construction began under the supervision of Prince Platon Zubov, the governor-general of the province of New Russia (Novorossiya) of which Odessa now formed a part. Because of the ravines dividing the city, De Voland laid out two gridirons intersecting at a 45-degree angle. To preserve uniform rectangularity in the city blocks, the principal gridiron had to be set at an angle to the shore. The plan provided for spacious streets one hundred feet wide. An esplanade separated the old Turkish fort from the residential area, forming a stately space overlooking the bluff to the water.

With the rapid rise of the new town on the southern fringe of the Russian Empire, young and beautiful Odessa appeared to emerge like Aphrodite from the foam of the Black Sea. One writer remarked, "Salt spray as stiff as whipped-up white of egg blew off the crest of the waves, and froth billowed and quivered on the beach; it was easy to believe the Greeks that it had given birth to Aphrodite."[5] Isaac Babel lovingly described his city as being on "the sun-drenched steppes washed by the sea."[6] Although Cath-

КУЯЛЬНИЦКІЙ Андреевскій ЛИМАНЪ

Г. ОДЕССА
ГРЯЗЕ-ЛИМАННОЕ ЛѢЧЕБНОЕ ЗАВЕДЕНІЕ
и САНАТОРІЯ

"VALETUDO"
Альвины Фрейндлихъ

ПРИ САНАТОРІИ ДВА ВРАЧА, СЕСТРЫ МИЛОСЕРДІЯ,
ФЕЛЬДШЕРИЦЫ, КОНСУЛЬТАЦІИ по ВСѢМЪ СПЕЦІАЛЬН.
СТРОГІЙ РЕЖИМЪ для РЕВМАТИКОВЪ и АРТРИТИКОВЪ.
ОТДѢЛЬНОЕ ПЕРВОКЛАСНОЕ ЗДАНІЕ для ГРЯЗЕВЫХЪ
и РАПНЫХЪ ВАННЪ
для ЛИЦЪ ЖИВУЩ.
въ САНАТОРІИ.
Завѣдывающій санаторіей
Др. Я. Р. МАРОВСКІЙ.

Spa advertisement.

erine had said she thought the capital of Russia should be on the Black Sea, not in Northern Russia, she never saw her creation, for she died in 1796, only two years after the official birthday of the city. She chose her architect and engineer well, however, in selecting De Voland and De Ribas. No doubt there were capable Russian engineers, but these two adventuresome and imaginative foreigners had participated in the conquest of the area and had an interest in its future.

De Ribas, effectively the head of the emerging city after 1793, became its first official *gradonachal'nik* (city chief) in January 1797. After the death of his patroness, Catherine, he was dismissed from his office, returned to St. Petersburg, became embroiled with the plot to assassinate Catherine's son, Paul I, and died in 1801, the same year as the murdered tsar.

Meanwhile, his younger brother Felix followed him into the Russian army, married a Polish woman, and after leaving the military, became a landowner, grain merchant, and entrepreneur by building a pasta factory in Odessa. Not wishing to become a Russian subject, he sought and received in 1807 the title of Odessa Consul for Sicily, then under Bourbon rule. For twenty years he sent commercial and political reports as well as personal letters to Naples, which, in a way, also represent the diary of his life in Odessa. One of the highlights of his official life was the visit of Queen Maria Carolina of Sicily to Odessa in 1813. But even this royal personage was subjected to a stay in the Quarantine, because the plague had visited Odessa the year before. As soon as she got out of Quarantine, she attended the Odessa theater.

Although Felix fell on hard times financially toward the end of his long life, he groomed his oldest son Michael to carry on the role of Consul for Sicily by training him in the Italian, French, Russian, and German languages. But the government of the Two Sicilies never gave him the coveted position. Young Michael had to be content with being appointed by his father as an unpaid vice-consul. Unlike his father, who was a merchant and industrialist, scholarly Michael composed the first short history of Odessa in 1834 in Italian. He later wrote various articles on geography and even a short story, but he admitted that he could not fully identify himself as either Neapolitan or Russian, only as an Odessite. As an Italian journalist once wrote, "In Odessa Russians feel a bit foreign and foreigners feel a bit Russian."[7] Michael De Ribas did finally become a Russian subject, a member of the city's Society for History and Antiquity, as well as the editor of one of Odessa's first newspapers, the *Journal d'Odessa*, published in French and Russian. Eventually, he became a bibliographer in Odessa's library.[8]

One of the De Ribas descendants, Alexander, fully acculturated as a Russian in Odessa, published in 1913 a history of the city and his own memoirs in Russian entitled *Old Odessa*.[9] As the writer Yuri Olesha recorded in his memoirs, "Alexander Mikhailovich Deribas was a respected man in Odessa, an expert on the city and its history, who had lived there a long time, and who, moreover, was the director of the Public Library. He was a tall old man with a long white beard, and when speaking, he shaped his lips in a manner that betrayed his provenance: he was French."[10] This vignette of the lives of the De Ribas family shows how this Spanish (not really French) family from Naples became true Odessites and how they contributed to the conquest, building, commerce, wealth, and intellectual life of the city of their adoption.

Many other foreigners came to Odessa to make a fortune in exporting the golden grain from the steppes. The most visible of these were the Greek émigrés who answered the siren call of the seaport. Within four years of the establishment of the city, at least forty-six Greek families resided in Odessa, which one Greek described as the land of "milk and honey" because trade flourished and the rule was mild. These prosperous families soon built their own Greek theater, commercial school, and benevolent societies. The Ralli, Rodokanaki, Scaramanga, Serafino, Mavrokordato, Iannopulo, Khristodulo, Mavros, Papudov, Zarifi, Paleologos,

Aviation school advertisement.

Inglesi, and Marazli families were among the pioneers in the grain trade. They took advantage of far-flung family members in Mediterranean and European seaports, Venice, Trieste, Livorno, Marseilles, and others for commercial intelligence and help in selling Russian grain to be transformed into French bread and Italian pasta. By 1832 most of the forty export firms in Odessa were in Greek hands, some worth as much as a million rubles, but most valued between 50,000 and 100,000 rubles.

Many of these wealthy Greeks enhanced Odessa's civic and cultural life.[11] Dmitrios Inglesi was mayor of the city from 1818 until 1821, and Grigory Marazli became mayor in 1879, serving for nearly a quarter of a century. During that period, he established forty social and educational institutions and made many municipal improvements. He shifted his family's commercial wealth into real estate and industry, a sign of the family's long-term commitment to the city. The tax register of 1873 shows that he owned more than a dozen pieces of choice real estate worth then about 300,000 rubles, or about 0.7 percent of the value of all the private buildings in Odessa. In 1899, he and several others, including Edmund G. Harris, an English engineer, applied to set up a joint-stock company in the construction business with offices in Odessa, Kherson, Bessarabia, Podolia, Ekaterinoslav, and Taurida. Thanks to the success of his many business ventures, he was able to indulge his generous impulses, such as subsidizing the publication of many books on Odessa's history. As mayor, he attempted to introduce electric lights to the city. With his own money he built a chapel in the Christian cemetery. He gave the city a neoclassical palace, built in 1828 by architect Francesco Buffo for Lev Alexandrovich Naryshkin, which is now a museum of art. Marazli also donated to the city another showplace, a French neoclassical mansion built in 1856 for the rich merchant Abaza. Since 1920, it has housed the Western and Eastern Arts Museum.

In 1883, Marazli engaged the architect Felix Gonsiorovsky to build a huge public library on Exchange Square, the first building constructed in Odessa specifically for public use. Today this Palladian palace houses the Archeological Museum. In 1892, Marazli built another enormous public reading room in the Greek revival style with two public schools attached, designed by Yu. M. Dmitrenko, also a gift to the city. These libraries served until 1904, when the city built a neoclassical library (now named for Maxim Gorky) on Pasteur Street. Marazli gave one of his dachas, located about four kilometers from the city, to the Odessa branch of the Imperial Horticultural Society, which was founded in 1884. Marazli's interest in science was reflected in his equipping the bacteriological laboratory in the city. This was the first of its kind in the empire; there, the Nobel Prize–winning scientist I. I. Mechnikov made his valuable experiments in microbiology. Today Odessa University is named for Mechnikov.

Marazli built a children's park in the Duc de Richelieu's Gardens for the poor children of the Moldavanka and Slobodka-Romanovka districts. He paid for an addition to the Sturdza Almshouse for children. In 1870, in memory of his mother, Zoe Theodorovna, he contributed five thousand rubles to support girls living in the Maria Theodorovna Orphanage. In 1892, he not only financed a retirement home for veterans, but also donated a large shelter for the homeless. Among his many charities were large subventions to the City Theater, especially to support Italian opera. Grateful to the "pearl of the Black Sea" that had conveyed wealth to the family, Marazli in turn enriched and adorned the city.

In addition to the riches promised by the "happy marriage" between the black earth grain-producing region and the Black Sea port, foreigners were attracted to Odessa because of its progressive administration. After valiant service fighting in the Russian army, the much beloved Frenchman Armand Emmanuel, Duc de Richelieu, related to the famous cardinal, ruled benignly and efficiently over the city from 1803 until his return to Paris as French foreign minister in 1814. Modest in his demeanor and in his material demands, hardworking, and devoted to the city, he carried the population through the plague in 1812 and fostered the grain trade in Odessa. His kindness and compassion enabled him to bring social harmony to the disparate people coming to live in the "Little Paris" so that both that Nogai Tatars and local Jews regarded him as a father. Clad in a toga atop a pedestal, the Duc's statue stands above the giant staircase overlooking the harbor, a continuing reminder of the genial governor-general who gave the city such a favorable start.

Richelieu was Odessa's "Johnny Appleseed." To anyone who promised to plant and tend them, he gave acacia trees, which he imported from Vienna and paid for himself. To colonists, he gave land if they promised to plant three hundred trees. Although the cliffs and seashore of Odessa were covered with broom and presented a lovely yellow face to the sailor, the terrain lacked trees. One of the Duc's legacies, the Primorsky Boulevard, an esplanade paralleling the sea cliff, is especially cool under the shade of acacias and inviting to strollers and those who would sit on benches to read, relax, or eye the passing promenaders.

Richelieu was succeeded by his friend and military companion, Louis Alexandre, Comte de Langeron, who headed the city's and region's administration until 1822. He was able to extract from the tsar free-port status for Odessa so that imports did not bear Russian tariffs. Writing back to France, he said, "All the territory entrusted to me is as large as all of France and is populated by ten different nationalities and by many foreigners. There are to be found also ten different religions and all ten are practiced freely. One can judge the work which burdens me and the absolute impossibility of my doing it all."[12] He must have been overworked or extremely absent-minded because when Tsar Alexander I, his patron, came to visit him and the city founded by his grandmother, Langeron inadvertently locked the tsar in the house. Apparently this mishap did not discourage Alexander's youngest brother Nicholas, the future Nicholas I, from spending four days with Langeron in Odessa: he was impressed by the vibrant city.

Langeron passed his retirement in St. Petersburg, where he died of cholera in 1831. It was said that as long as he was in Odessa, he never learned the Russian language, although he married a Russian princess, Trubetskaya.

Another noble presided over the city's growth and fortunes for over thirty years, Count Mikhail S. Vorontsov, who was appointed governor-general of New Russia in 1823. Although he spent his youth in London, where his father was Russian ambassador to the Court of St. James and one of his contemporaries sniffed, "he is more an English lord than a Russian dignitary," he was a Russian. Dedicated to his work as caretaker of the city and region, honest and liberal, he was also, like the Duc de Richelieu, tolerant of all the ethnic groups and religious groups he governed. Jews hailed him as their benefactor. Under his guidance the archeological museum opened in 1825. In 1828, he founded the Imperial Agricultural Society for Southern Russia in the city, and about a decade later, he helped to found the Imperial Odessa Society of History and Antiquities. He also founded the newspapers *Odessa Herald* and the *New Russian Calendar*. In short, he was a worthy successor to the Duc and his statue still stands in Cathedral Square. The Bolsheviks left it intact, although they tore down the cathedral and a monument to Catherine II.

That his memory is as solid as his statue was shown at the two hundredth anniversary of the city when the Odessa composer Oleksandr Krastov premiered his opera *Mikhail Vorontsov*, as part of the celebrations of 1994. Vorontsov also left us his memoirs, a valuable historical source. Vorontsov was followed as head of Odessa and New Russia by Count Alexander G. Stroganov, a wealthy, wise, and tolerant leader. He also worked hard to improve municipal services such as gaslights, street paving, waterworks, and bridge building. He was one of the founders of the New Russian University, to which he bequeathed his library of 14,000 books that are still available to the reader with some of his notations in the margins. He pressed for the emancipation of the serfs, the building of railroads in the vicinity (here he was unsuccessful), and the founding of the Russian Steam Navigation and Trading Company for commerce on the Black Sea. Under his successor, Adjutant General Pavel E. Kotsebu, Odessa finally had a railroad connection and city improvements speeded up. Kotsebu founded an eye hospital and an asylum for orphans, later named "Pavlov" for him. The American consul in Odessa reported that he was a very popular governor-general who was able to extract favors for the city from the tsar.

After the transfer of Kotsebu in 1874 to Warsaw, Odessa was never to enjoy the personal favors of the tsars again. The early noble governors-general had been close friends of the monarchs they served and, since they took an intense interest and pride in developing the city, they had won concessions such as free-port status and money from the royal purse for the city's infrastructure and cultural institutions. With the advent of municipal government in 1863, there were some sincere and hardworking heads of the city, but they did not have close ties with the throne. Many members of the city council suffered not only from apathy, but often from a reluctance to tax themselves for the benefit of the city. Progress was much slower, and sometimes absent altogether. Odessa grew in the third quarter of the nineteenth century, but it was no longer the darling of the tsars.

Nonetheless, the city's population growth was phenomenal, beginning with little over 2,000 persons in 1795, to 35,000 in 1815, and reaching 116,000 in 1861. According to the 1897 census, the population was over 400,000, growing at rates on a par with some western cities in America. The growth came from the continual stream of immigrants from within the empire and from abroad, which made Odessa a boomtown, where as late as 1892 only 45 percent of the population had been born there.

By 1892, many of the early foreign immigrants—Greeks, Italians, Jews, Ukrainians, Poles, Tatars, Armenians, Belorussians, Mordvinians, and Georgians—had become Russian subjects and

Advertisement for Artistic and Industrial Exhibition 1910.

Car advertisement.

were no longer counted among the foreign population. Russification of the city came slowly, however. As one traveler observed, Odessa possessed "Italian houses, Russian officials, French ships, and German artisans." Even the Duc de Richelieu, noting that so little Russian was spoken in the city, ordered the high school he founded to teach the Russian language. By 1892, the number of foreign non-subjects was 7 percent of the population, a much larger percentage than in Moscow (0.75 percent) or even St. Petersburg, the much vaunted "Window to the West," whose foreigners constituted only 2.35 percent of its population. Odessa's colorful mix of population stamped the character of the city at least until the 1917 revolution.

A native of the city, born in 1880, made this observation:

> Even if it was a city in Russia and in my time very russified in language, Odessa was not a Russian city. Nor was it a Jewish city, though Jews were probably the largest ethnic community, particularly when one takes into account that half of the so-called Russians were actually Ukrainians, a people just as different from the Russians as Americans from Britons, or Englishmen from Irishmen. At least four great peoples—three ancient ones, and the fourth a young one—united to build the city: first the Greeks and Italians, a little later came the Jews, and only in the 1840s did the actual Russian influence begin to grow. The city was also full of Poles, Armenians, Caucasians, Tatars, Moldavians, and a half dozen other peoples. In Odessa everybody was an Odessan and everyone who was literate read the same newspapers and thought about the same Russian problems.[13]

A census tells us where these foreign residents of the city were from as of 1892. About 24 percent came from Turkey, 20 percent from Greece, 18 percent from Austria-Hungary, and 13 percent from Germany, and, in descending order, from Romania, Italy,

France, Great Britain, Slavic countries, Switzerland, Persia, Belgium, Sweden and Norway, Spain, Denmark, the United States, and the Low Countries. People from all these countries lived in Odessa and were not tourists whose numbers go unrecorded. No other city in the Russian Empire hosted such a variety of people. Although economic opportunities undoubtedly brought them to the commercial seaport, the climate, cultural amenities, ambiance, and aesthetic enjoyment of the site help to explain why they remained in Odessa. No doubt each of these various ethnic groups contributed to the exotic flavor of the city, but since it bore a foreign imprint from the start, they often found congenial surroundings when they arrived.

Vladimir Jabotinsky, born in Odessa in 1880, a Zionist after the 1903 pogroms in Kishinev, provided his own distinct history of the various people who came to Odessa:

> From the hundreds of cities of Italy, from Genoa to Brindisi, a long procession of dark-eyed adventurers made their way towards Odessa: merchants, shipbuilders, architects, and smugglers of the choicest variety. They populated the young capital and gave it their language, their light-hearted music, their style of building and laid down the basis of its future wealth. At approximately the same time the Greeks started pouring into Odessa, shopkeepers, boatmen and also, of course, masters of illicit trades. These connected the young port of Odessa with every nook and cranny of the Anatolian coast, with the Aegean Isles, with Smyrna and other ports.
>
> Then came Jews, who cut into the steppes a cobweb of invisible canals down which harvests from the rich Ukraine poured into Odessa. Thus Odessa was built by the descendants of the three tribes, which once created humanity: the Greeks, the Romans, and the Jews. Later came Russians and Ukrainians. The Russians ruled.[4]

As for the Ukrainians, Jabotinsky wrote, "they gave Odessa her superb sailors and masons and—most important—the salt of the earth, those pillars of the fatherland, those real creators of Odessa and of the whole of south Russia—those real, full-blooded human beings: I mean, of course the tramps." Again, in his chronology, afterwards came Turks and French and Armenians. In 1892, 58 percent of Odessa's population was ethnically non-Russian. It was the people of all of these nations and their cultures, richly interwoven, who together built Jabotinsky's birthplace "under the laughing sun, among the smells of the sea, of acacia and garlic, my town, the genuine and legitimate child though born before its mother—of a League of Nations."

These immigrants saw beautiful public and even private buildings designed by some of the empire's leading architects. While Odessa's buildings were stately and substantial, they were not monumental except for the Opera House. They were built to a human scale, and the center presented a harmonious ensemble to the eye. As early as 1809 the neoclassical court architect Thomas de Thomon of St. Petersburg completed two beautiful edifices in the city, the theater and the hospital. Two local architects of Italian origin, Francesco Frappoli and Francesco Boffo, also worked on the theater, so that Europeans would find familiar façades when coming to Odessa, where, in fact, were some of the finest in Russia.

Other artists came from St. Petersburg as well: the architects A. I. Mel'nikov and Auguste Montferrand, and the sculptor I. Martos. In 1829, the city had an Exchange built by a local architect, G. Toricelli, following the plans, according to some and disputed by others, of the famous St. Petersburg architect Giacomo Quarenghi. At the time of its completion in 1834, it was a showy neoclassical building located at the southern end of the Primorsky Boulevard on the top of the cliff looking over the Black Sea.

At the entrance of the building were two rows of Corinthian

Engraving of the founding of Odessa, 1794.

columns, which led out from a covered courtyard that served as a place for trading operations. The composition and the style were reminiscent of the Alexandrovsky Palace in Tsarskoe Selo near St. Petersburg—not surprisingly, since the latter was also designed by Quarenghi. It cost the city 65,000 rubles to build, but private funds were used as well as public. In 1871, the architect F. O. Morandi rebuilt the edifice, the city's first Exchange or *Birzha*, converting the covered courtyard into a hall; he also tore down a second row of columns. Nonetheless, the building did not lose its architectural importance nor its beautifully proportioned first row of columns. In the second half of the nineteenth century when the New Exchange was built, the earlier *birzha* became the home of the City Duma.

At the northern end of the Primorsky Boulevard was another and even larger classical building, the palace of Count Vorontsov, constructed in 1828, according to the plans of Francesco K. Boffo. Vorontsov chose to erect it at the spot where the Duc de Richelieu had occupied a modest little house in the early days of the city. The most striking part of the palace is a detached portico of twenty semicircular Doric columns facing the sea that makes it the most easily observed landmark even at a distance for those coming to the city by water. It is prominent enough to serve as a landmark from various vantage points in the city as well. After the Revolution of 1905, it became the home of an engineering school. In Soviet times Vorontsov's home became the Palace of Pioneers, and during the Romanian occupation (1941 to 1944), it was the home of the governor.

Thomas de Thomon's first construction in Odessa was a massive classical building at the start of Pasteur Street erected in 1806–7, a two-story building which was the first city hospital. Two adjoining curved wings were added in 1821, surrounded by a six-columned portico. Almost at the same time, he designed the first Odessa Opera House, which burned in 1873. He also built stately granaries at the port, which appeared to be palaces that were perhaps unique to Odessa since they elicited so many comments from visitors to the city.

No discussion of the architecture of Odessa would be complete without at least reference to the gigantic stairway leading from Primorsky Boulevard down to the port, the source of most of the city's wealth. It was designed by Francesco Boffo, the architect of the commune of Odessa from 1822 to 1844. Construction began in 1837 and was completed in 1842. Contemporaries called it the grand staircase but now it is better known as the Potemkin Steps, so named for the famous scene in Eisenstein's film *The Battleship Potemkin*. The staircase is still one of the most dramatic sights of the city, whether looking up from the port or down on the staircase from Primorsky Boulevard. Before the Soviet period, there was a funicular alongside the staircase, which the Soviets tore down and later built a garish escalator in its place. (Happily, a funicular will occupy its old place in the near future.)

Одесса. — Соборная площадь.
Odessa. — Place de Cathédrale.

Cathedral Square. Postcard, early 1910s.

At the top of the staircase stands the statue of the Duc de Richelieu sculpted by Ivan Petrovich Martos in 1827. Behind the statue and built about the same time in the center of Primorsky Boulevard are two semicircular buildings whose architect was Francesco Boffo, but whose final elaboration belongs to the well-known architect A. I. Mel'nikov from St. Petersburg. Among the most handsome edifices in the city, they frame the top of the staircase and the opening of Ekaterininskaya Street like parentheses, leading to the center of town. One of the curved buildings served as a hotel; the other was an office for city administrators. Ekaterininskaya was one of the main streets of Odessa that flowed into town from the grand staircase.

In 1830, Boffo also designed a handsome neoclassical building on Primorsky Boulevard for M. N. Shidlovsky, who later was governor-general of the city (1865 to 1868). In 1835, Countess M. A. Naryshkina became the owner of the building. Rebuilt after the Second World War, it became the home of the Seaman's Club.

Boffo created the "marine façade" of the city, that is, the buildings along Primorsky Boulevard, the Potemkin Steps, and the concept of the statue of Richelieu. Governor-General Vorontsov nominated him in 1828 for the prize of the Order of St. Vladimir, Fourth Class, for which Boffo became a member of the Russian hereditary nobility. Even during the reign of Nicholas I (1825–55), Odessa's architecture continued to reflect a classical style. That is, until Nicholas began to favor pseudo-gothic architecture in St. Petersburg, so that in Odessa, too, private individuals built large houses in the pseudo-gothic style along the seashore. Although suburbs developed, the growth of population on the whole created a denser center city rather than urban sprawl. In 1849, the architect F. O. Morandi drew up a new master plan for the city in which all buildings had to conform to prescribed imperial plans for façades, which were essentially neoclassical in style. Not until the latter half of the century was more eclecticism displayed in the designing of buildings.

The new City Theater (Opera House), begun in 1883 and completed in 1887 at the cost of 1.3 million rubles, was designed in the Italian Renaissance and Baroque style by two Viennese architects, Ferdinand Fellner and Hermann Helmer, who designed over seventy theaters during the last quarter of the nineteenth century and the twentieth up until World War I, principally in Eastern Europe. It is, after the Potemkin Steps, the most famous edifice in the city and certainly exceedingly grand. In the exterior niches of the Opera House are busts of Pushkin, Gogol, Griboyedov, and Glinka. The large hall, in the style of Louis XVI, was richly decorated with gilded stucco design and figures. Frescos on the ceiling depicted various Shakespearean scenes. In addition to the wide parterre, there were four tiers of loges, a dress circle, a balcony, and a gallery. The theater is located near the Primorsky Boulevard.

On October 13, 1887, at the opening of the new theater, the music-mad Odessa public was treated to a performance of excerpts from *Boris Godunov* by Mussorgsky and the third act of Griboye-

ОДЕССА.—ODESSA. № 102.
Домъ трудолюбія.—La maison d'industrie.

Church at the House of Industriousness. Lithograph, early 1900s.

dov's play, *Woe from Wit.* The theater was illuminated by electricity, making it the first building in Odessa to employ the Edison Company. Unfortunately, there was a fire in 1925, but the building was restored and then later remodeled in the 1960s. Disastrously, the huge edifice sits atop shifting ground and is in danger of collapsing. A former opera singer in the theater, who happened to be trained as a geologist, is helping to advise on how the building can be saved, a costly enterprise.

That the imposing theater, often used as an opera house, occupied considerable space and resources is indicative of how much Odessites loved music, and still do. Apparently, the large Italian merchant community in the city provided the first impetus to produce Italian opera. But soon the entire city became enamored of the productions. It was said even Ukrainian grain carters were heard whistling Italian arias in the streets of Odessa. And a Russian declared that Jews were fanatics of the Italian opera, and indeed their attendance confirms their enthusiasm. Pinkhas Minkovsky, a cantor in Odessa, claimed that the reason that Odessa

became such a strong center for cantorial music was because Jews were immersed in music.[15]

Beggars were supposedly happier in Odessa than elsewhere because they were surrounded by music. In Odessa, the fictional vagrant Fiske exclaimed:

> well, you might even say that barrel organs has gone over mighty big in Odessa as a general thing. I mean you can't turn a corner anywheres, indoors or out, without you got a barrel organ or some such wheezebox grinding away at you there. Barrel organs in the street, barrel organs at home, barrel organs in taverns, barrel organs at the circus . . . they even got the shameless gumption to be playing them things at shul![16]

Alexander Kuprin uses music as a mirror to reflect changing times and political moods of the city in his famous short story "Gambrinus," in which Sasha the Jewish musician plays military marches, revolutionary tunes, and merry dance tunes. After the police brutally mutilate his arm so that he can no longer play the fiddle, he triumphantly plays a flute.[17]

A newspaper, *Troubadour d'Odessa,* founded in 1822, was devoted to news of the theater, the opera, and other musical events. It included scores and lyrics for operas and musical scores for piano, harp, and guitar. During the early years of the theater, operas, ballets, and vaudeville shows were staged in Italian, French, and Russian. But during the 1820s and 1830s, Italian opera predominated. As a music historian noted, "the earliest more or less continuous Italian opera enterprise in nineteenth century Russia was based in neither capital, but in the Black Sea port city of Odessa, where a state theater for opera and ballet was opened in 1809."[18] When the great Russian poet Alexander Pushkin was sent in exile to Odessa in the early 1820s, he was delighted to engage in the cultural life of the growing city. In his masterful poem *Eugene Onegin*, he speaks of the dusty streets of Odessa and of its colorful polyglot population. He was an enthusiastic fan of the impresario Luigi Buonavoglia and his company. Pushkin, writing to a friend, noted "in the evenings I don't go anywhere except to the theater." Pushkin mentioned Rossini's operas of which eight were performed before the poet was evicted from the city. Pushkin might have remained longer had he not flirted with Governor Vorontsov's wife.

In 1824, the impresario Cesare Negri signed a three-year contract for 38,000 rubles in addition to a 12,000-ruble subvention for his passage from Italy to put on eighty-six performances per year in Odessa. The poet and Polish patriot Adam Mickiewicz was a patron, and the Russian poet Konstantin Batyushkov pronounced Odessa's theater to be superior to that of Moscow. A German visitor to the Opera House in the 1840s was impressed that performances were given in five different languages.[19] Even while Vorontsov was city chief, he and his wife, as well as other aristocrats, invited chamber music groups to perform in their salons. By 1842, the Philharmonic Society of Odessa was founded. In February 1860, A. A. Tedesco formed Odessa's first symphony orchestra, and in the following year the first important program featured music by Russian composers. In 1864, the Society of Music Lovers was established in the city.

In 1834, Italians established the first music school. Violin classes at the school began in 1848. The pianist D. von Ressel, supported by the composer-pianist Anton Rubinstein, opened a branch of the Imperial Russian Musical Society in Odessa in 1866. The first concert, conducted by W. Kaulbars, featured music by Felix Mendelssohn and Robert Schumann. In 1889, Rubinstein himself played to celebrate the twenty-fifth anniversary of the society. This sparkling event was held in the New Bourse, or Exchange, which to this day is the home of the Odessa Philharmonic Orchestra. During the first quarter-century of the music

View of the city from Ekaterinskaya Yacht Club. Postcard, early 1910s.

society, they gave eighty-two symphony concerts. A German choir of local colonists regularly sang before the group. The Odessa Conservatory was established in 1913. Odessa was filled with music. Even the Reformed and Lutheran churches put on beautiful concerts of religious music. Music-loving Odessa Jews shocked conservatives by insisting that an organ be placed in their synagogue.

As Steven J. Zipperstein has noted, "The manifestation of a widespread interest in, and even a gift for, music on the part of Odessa Jews in the first half of the nineteenth century is intriguing, particularly in view of the large number of famous Jewish violinists, such as Mischa Elman and David Oistrakh, to emerge from Odessa several decades later."[20] The great violinist David Oistrakh was born in Odessa in 1908, studied at the Odessa Conservatory, and eventually went on world tours demonstrating his genius. According to one of his Odessa friends, Mark Zinger, when Oistrakh returned to Odessa in 1968 to give a concert, he insisted on going out for three hours to photograph his native city in colored film. In addition to taking the usual pictures of notable streets and monuments, he took pictures of P. S. Stolyarsky's home and then even his dacha, a loving tribute of a famous pupil to his first teacher.

Mischa Elman, another violin prodigy, known to Bel Kaufman and her family, was a local genius. In his autobiographical story "The Awakening," Babel wrote:

> All the people of our circle—middlemen, storekeepers, clerks in banks and steamship offices—sent their children to music lessons. Our fathers, seeing they had no prospects of their own, set up a lottery for themselves. They built this lottery on the bones of their little children. Odessa was in the grip of this craze more than any other town. And sure enough, over the last few decades our town had sent a number of child prodigies onto the stages of the world. Mischa Elman, Zimbalist, Gawrilowitsch all came from Odessa—Jascha Heifetz started out with us. When a boy turned four or five, his mother took the tiny, frail creature to Mr. Zagursky [Stolyarsky]. Zagursky ran a factory that churned out child prodigies, a factory of Jewish dwarfs in lace collars and patent leather shoes. He went hunting for them in the Moldavanka slums and the reeking courtyards of the old bazaar. Zagursky gave them the first push, then the children were sent off to Professor Auer in St. Petersburg.[21]

Babel continued by saying that his father decided when Isaac was fourteen that he too should become a prodigy and sent him to Stolyarsky for violin lessons. But "the sounds scraped out of my violin like iron filings. These sounds cut even into my own heart, but my father would not give up. All anyone talked about at home was Mischa Elman."[22] Young Babel decided to skip the lessons to play at the beach. When finally the music teacher informed the family of Isaac's truancy, the boy had to lock himself in the lavatory against his father's rage in losing "the lottery." His aunt set him free during the night to take him to the safety of his grandmother's house.

Peter (Peisakh) Stolyarsky, a native of Odessa, was one of the founders of the violin school. He devised a method to teach young children how to play and by 1923 was a professor of the Odessa Conservatory. As the world now knows, Babel's music was in his prose. And while he never became a musician, he delighted in attending the theater, which was very popular in Odessa in the early twentieth century. Babel described how, as a young man, he loved seeing the Sicilian tragic actor Di Grasso in *King Lear* and *Othello*, noting that scalpers obtained five times the regular price of tickets.[23]

Over the years, great names appeared on the Odessa stage, such as composer-conductors Tchaikovsky, Rubinstein, Rimsky-Korsakov, Napravnik, Arensky, and Glazunov. In 1847, Franz Liszt played six triumphant piano concerts in the theater. The Odessa pianist Svyatoslav Richter was self-taught. At the age of eighteen he was the accompanist and assistant conductor of the Odessa Opera, making his first solo concert debut in Odessa in 1935. Opera directors included the Italians Montovani and Zamboni. Famous singers also performed: Fedor Chalyapin, Enrico Caruso, Mattia Battistini, Giuseppe Anselmi, and Titta Ruffo. The Italian singer Moriconi came directly to Odessa when she finished the conservatory in Turin. She sang not only popular Italian operas, but became interested in Russian folk songs, learned Russian, and sang in Russian while appearing in Russian costumes. So while Russians were becoming Italian opera fans, Italian opera singers became fascinated with Russian music.

Other Italian divas appeared as well, such as Caterina Amati and Adelanda Rinaldi, who earned as much as 500 rubles per month, a sizable sum compared with the 300 rubles earned by conductor and first violinist Sankte-Campioni. So engrossed in opera were music lovers that entire factions would form around particular divas; fans would sometimes come to blows with those supporting rival Italian singing stars. In fact, by 1911, the Opera House (see page 38) was staging more and more opera and less theater. In the 1920s and 1930s productions became experimental, borrowing much from avant-garde cinema.

Why was Odessa so amply endowed with talented musical performers and appreciative audiences? Some have noted that one factor was geography. That relatively southern spot attracted from southern climates ethnic groups already famous for playing musical instruments and singing: Ukrainians, Jews, gypsies, Armenians, Italians, and southern Russians. As early as the 1820s, musicians from various nationalities organized musical unions or guilds (*tsekh muzykantov*) to perform at weddings, funerals, gala birthday parties, and other functions. If one studies carefully the 1894 photo collage on page 52, it can be seen that dignitaries at the top, Catherine the Great and the famous governors of the region and city, stand proudly with their medals, epaulets, and ribbons around Mother Russia with Infant Odessa on her lap (almost like the Madonna with Child). The common people at the bottom, mostly children, carry folk musical instruments: an Italian girl with a violin, a German girl with a guitar, a Polish girl with a lute, an Albanian girl with a triangle, a Ukrainian girl with a *domra*, and a Russian boy with a flute. It is significant that the picture assembled to represent the accomplishments of the city over a hundred years should feature so predominately musical instruments.

On the other hand, the most democratic and widely used instrument was the violin. Self-taught violin virtuosos were mostly Jews, gypsies, and Ukrainians. The typical Ukrainian ensemble *(troïsti muziki)* was, and is, a trio: two fiddles and a flute. They never sang, only accompanied Ukrainian folk dancers. And of course, no Jewish celebration would be complete without a fiddler for dancers. Gypsy violinists often accompanied their own soloist

singer. Thus child prodigy musicians and virtuosi were relatively rare, even in Odessa, compared with the large numbers of people who produced and enjoyed music in that city with its soft inviting summers and autumns that encouraged people to dance, sing, and play music outdoors, a tradition that continues today with its outdoor cafés, bands, and even karaoke concerts.

The popular Soviet Odessa singer and bandleader of the 1920s, Leonid Utesov (L. I. Vaisbein), wrote in his memoirs about a piece he performed called "How Bands Play at Weddings in Odessa." He claimed that in Odessa, groups of musicians, *klezmorim* (probably following the old tradition of musical unions or guilds), who could not read music, showed up at ordinary weddings and functioned as a collection of soloists, producing music, "in an original, freely improvised style" (see page 33). He went on to claim that "this curious manner of playing was then widely used in America some ten or fifteen years later by small amateur Negro bands in New Orleans. Like the poor Odessa musicians, the New Orleans amateurs did not use scores. They varied the themes of well-known melodies freely, and at times with inspiration."[24] He concluded, in effect, that jazz was invented in Odessa, not New Orleans. This claim was made as part of a comic routine and thus in jest, but foreigners took it seriously.[25] This was, after all, the man who proudly said that Odessa should not be compared to Paris, for Paris should shine Odessa's shoes. His own chosen name Utesov comes from *utes*, meaning cliff, after the city's site. And the first lines of his memoirs are, "I was born in Odessa. You think I am bragging? But it's really true. Many people would like to have been born in Odessa, but not everyone manages to."[26] Or as the cinematographer Kozak recently observed, whenever one informs others that he or she was born in Odessa, a smile comes to their lips and they mention, "Odessa humor, Odessa songs, Odessa jokes, and the characteristic Odessa speech. An Odessite is without fail, merry, witty, sharp; he is never despondent, petty; he has a superior and fascinating personality."[27]

However valid Utesov's claim to Odessa's inventing jazz might be, the city has always patronized jazz players, including Peter Rozenkern's band of the 1930s that based much of its jazz music on lusty ballads from the Moldavanka Jewish district. Sooner or later, there was a blend of Yiddish music and jazz in Odessa. As Richard Stites noted, "the strains of an Odessa Jewish wedding were never far away [from jazz]."[28] Utesov's film, *Happy-Go-Lucky Guys*, also known as *Jolly Fellows*, of the 1930s was extremely popular. It reflected his European style as a typical Estrada entertainer— quick witted, versatile, and funny. In 2001, Odessa placed a seated statue of Utesov on a bench, leaving room for someone to sit beside him. Nearby a machine plays songs sung by Utesov.

In 1916, Babel conceded that Odessa chanteuses "might not have much in the way of a voice, but they have a joy, an expressive joy, mixed with passion, lightness, and a touching charming, sad feeling for life. A life that is good, terrible, and *quand même et malgré tout*, exceedingly interesting."[29] Some of the better-known songs from Odessa, mostly sung in Yiddish, reveal the special characteristics of the city, like "Odessa Mama," in which some of the lyrics run, "What is Vienna or Paris to me. They're nothing, a travesty, no comparison, but Odessa—there you have a paradise, I tell you."[30] Another Yiddish song, "Akh, Odessa," proclaims: "there is only one of you, Odessa, in the whole world. Anyone who has not yet been in the beautiful city of Odessa hasn't seen the world

Cafe at Alexander Park. Postcard, early 1910s.

at all, and he has no idea of progress."[31] Even Odessa folk songs sung in Russian include Jewish figures such as in "A Beer Hall Opened on Deribaskovskaya," "The School of Ballroom Dancing," "The Story of the Kakhovka Rabbi," and "It's Terribly Noisy at Shneerson's House," in which the lyrics describe Abe the milkman and three of his brothers taking up instruments and constituting themselves into an impromptu jazz band.[32] The great modern balladeer, Vladimir Vysotsky, although he was not from the city, is said to have adopted the Odessa style of singing as well as Odessa songs.

Writing about the importance of music and comedy for the city, Stites noted that "Odessa exported its comedy and song patterns to Moscow. Odessa became renowned as a breeding ground for satirists, among whom Jews were especially prominent. But they dealt far more often with infidelity, high fashion, and in-laws than they did with tsarist repression."[33]

Odessites are renowned for their sense of humor, for their stand-up comics, some of whom have become popular in the United States. People recognize that these performers come from Odessa because of their Jewish intonations and gestures. Humor and music abounded in Odessa, but the inhabitants could be tough as well. Noted writer Konstantin Paustovsky described the role Odessites played in the First World War: "During the war the frivolous, garrulous Odessans, amateurs of comic songs and known as 'babbling brooks,' fought with grim courage—though they still cracked Odessan jokes—and showed such daring and selflessness that even the enemy were astonished."[34]

He continued by saying, "New songs came after the war, celebrating their feats and their unwavering love of their city." Music also marked the Civil War and NEP periods in Odessa, where "the most popular unofficial song of the twenties "Bublichki" ("Pretzels" or "Bagels") was written by Yakov Yadov for an Odessa cabaret. Its lyrics about a drunken father and a whoring mother were later adapted to an indecent underground parody song on the Bolshevik Civil War hero, V. I. Chapayev.[35] All through the 1920s musicians such as Leonid Utesov, who were later canonized as Soviet culture heroes, cranked out songs about Odessa thieves and jailbirds.[36] An eyewitness of the 1917 Revolution and the Civil War, Paustovsky also remarked that "there was an orchestra here, in Odessa. They called it the Roumanian orchestra but really it was made up of people of every sort—some from the Caucasus, some from Kishinev, and some from our Moldavanka."[37]

Entertainment was always prized in Odessa, whether it was opera, drama, comedy, or the circus. There was a long tradition of the circus in the city. In the early twentieth century Olesha was fascinated by it and as a boy often went without lunch and solicited extra kopecks from his grandmother to come up with the student fee of 50 kopecks. He described his joy:

> The circus was always seen through a curtain of falling snow. Well, why not, since it was always winter when the circus came! I walked through the falling snow, marveling at the snowflakes. On the circus building hung wall posters with a picture of yellow lions and a lion tamer in red, a picture that moved, I thought, for it contained rings and a cracking whip and lions whose hind legs were thrust into the air. . . . The lit-up wall, the poster. I read the words that would, in ten minutes, as soon as the lights in the arena were turned on, be converted into

clowns and mandolins and little dogs, into tambourines and horses and slender bodies, hurtling through the air between trapezes. . . . As a boy, and for many years afterward as an adult, of all entertainments, I was fondest of the circus.[38]

Odessites also loved going to movies. With twenty-five theaters in 1913, Odessa was third after St. Petersburg and Kiev in its number of movie houses. Because of the relatively mild weather in the area and the beautiful light, it was a good place for making movies as well, even after the 1917 Revolution, although during the Civil War the Odessa Studio was evacuated to the Crimea, the Caucasus, and Central Asia. Nikita Mikhailkov's popular 1970 movie, *Slave of Love*, was about moviemaking in the Odessa area before the revolution. It captured the lush scenery and beautiful light of the South. It happened that the great screen star Vera Kholodnaia died in Odessa in 1919 of the Spanish flu at the age of twenty-six. At the peak of her career, she was said to light up the screen with her luminosity in such movies as *The Last Tango* (1918), *Life for Life* (1916), *Children of the Age* (1915), and many more melodramas. There remain fragments of a newsreel of her funeral, which made her even more of a cult figure. The French comic Max Linder was also all the rage in Odessa. Sergei Eisenstein's famous 1925 silent film, *The Battleship Potemkin*, has become a classic, and through this movie millions have formed their visual images of the seaport.

As a seaport, Odessa was a melting pot. Not only did Odessa music blend Yiddish and Russian words, folk themes, and characters, but also each language absorbed a bit of the other and affected the other's syntax, lexicon, and phraseology. According to Babel, his grandmother mixed Polish and Hebrew words in with her Russian.[39] Perhaps that fact led him to state: "Odessa is a horrible town. It's common knowledge. Instead of saying 'a great difference,' people here say 'two great differences,' and 'tuda i syuda,' they pronounce 'tudoyu i syudoyu'! And yet I feel that there are quite a few good things one can say about this important town, the most charming city of the Russian Empire."[40]

According to the noted linguistics scholar Robert A. Rothstein, the Ukrainian language has also altered the Russian use of some prepositions to accord with Ukrainian usage. For a long time Odessites used the French forms of address *monsieur* and *madame*, and in 1895 a journalist proclaimed that the language of Odessa was "not even a language, but a language salad."[41] It is only natural that this city where so many languages were spoken would produce a kind of dialect of its own, or at least a nonstandard Russian that deviated from classical Russian in both pronunciation and vocabulary. Babel called it simply "Odessa's hot, homegrown lingo."[42] So distinct is the language of Odessa that there is a website devoted to it on the Internet, called "Odessa Language Dictionary" *(www.odessit.com).*

One of Odessa's chief cultural legacies is the rich Jewish and Yiddish literature generated in Odessa, read by all Odessan society, and now the world. Isaac Babel and Sholom Aleichem are among the most famous of the writers. Although Babel's *The Red Cavalry* is his masterpiece, his *Odessa Stories* provide an indelible picture of Odessa and its Jewish Moldavanka district. Thoroughly trained in biblical studies and in French, Babel wrote his early pieces in French and retained the storytelling style of Flaubert and Maupassant. Although he was influenced by Odessa's Yiddish writers, such as Mendele Mocher Sforim, he wrote his stories in Russian (including Odessa slang, ungrammatical Russian, and Yiddishisms) about very distinctive Jewish characters, most of whom are gangsters.

The leading bandit in these stories, Benya Krik, is modeled after a real-life gangster, Mishka Yaponchik (Mikhail Vinnisky), who is said to have been a veteran of the Russo-Japanese War (1904–5), and married to a Japanese woman (hence his sobriquet).

After serving time in prison, Yaponchik joined various groups—Bolsheviks, anarchists, and the anti-pogrom Jewish defense league. A writer living in Odessa during the Civil War wrote, "Three thousand bandits from the slums of Moldavanka with Misha the Jap at their head, looted half-heartedly. They were sated with fabulous loot from their previous raids. All they wanted was to relax from this strenuous occupation."[43] The situations described, mostly raids that took place when extortion money was not forthcoming, were all too real during the chaotic period of World War I and its aftermath, a time that witnessed brazen robberies in the city.

But even raids had a history in Odessa when political groups and individuals stole gold and other valuables from the state during the 1905 Revolution. Gangsters, thieves, and criminal types are celebrated in Odessan underworld songs such as "Music Is Playing in Moldavanka" or "Kal'ka the Pickpocket," "From the Odessa Jail," and "Murka," in which a bandit speaks of justice when he murders a fellow bandit because she might endanger their safety. A special code of honor and sense of legality pervades these songs and tales. Such underground songs *(blatnye pesni)* and Babel's stories derive from common Odessa legends in which violence takes a form of revelry. Babel's Jewish gangsters, therefore, followed a long tradition and heralded a continuation of that tradition celebrating those who defied the law in Odessa.

During the 1920s and 1930s, Il'f and Petrov, writers from Odessa, created Ostap Bender, if not an outright criminal, at least a crafty and cool rogue who outwits his adversaries. His exploits are also stinging critiques of the New Economic Program and the first Five-Year Plan. The 1989 Odessa movie *Déjà vu* is also a spoof of the NEP era in Odessa with its jazz, bootlegging, and sex.[44]

Always a kind of free city with free spirits, Odessa as a free port between 1817 and 1859 presented a temptation to smugglers, who would risk carrying duty-free goods to the interior. Since Odessa was built on quarried limestone used to construct the city, the honeycombed underground tunnels were ideal hiding places for *contrabandisti* throughout the first half of the nineteenth century. Smuggling continued even after the abolition of the free port in 1859. Paustovsky wrote that in Odessa just before the First World War one could obtain tobacco from Constantinople that seemed to be pure shredded gold as well as "French cocaine, Greek vodka, Messina oranges of exceptional flavor and aroma."[45] Babel's list of contraband was similar: "cigars, delicate silks, cocaine, and metal jiggers, uncut tobacco from the state of Virginia and black wine bought on the Island of Chios."[46]

As a rough seaport, Odessa was famed for its criminals. One visitor noted that there were "adventurers and swindlers of the most ruthless kind, people who had learned their lessons in scoundrelism at Constantinople, Romania, and the Levant, and had grown grey in vices and crimes of every description."[47] According to another, "Odessa turned out the most talented thieves in the world, certainly more ingenious, dexterous, and brazen than the Warsaw ones." And according to Roshanna P. Sylvester, Moldavanka criminals included many specialists: "gentlemen" pickpockets who operated in fancy stores, theaters, restaurants, lecture and meeting halls, banks, post offices, the stock exchange, and in expensive hotels; "Saturday and Sunday men" who cruised the weekend crowds on the main streets; "cleaners" who offered to dust off gentlemen's coats while lifting wallets; and "sinners" who specialized in stealing purses in churches. Other specialists were shoplifters, counterfeiters, falsifiers of gold watches, con artists of every description, as well as second-story burglars.[48]

In the 1870s, a Russian visitor to Odessa declared, "this town has degenerated into a focus of crime and dissolute excess, such as none of the governors-general, town prefects, or heads of police sent from St. Petersburg had even been able to master. Frauds and thefts of unprecedented extent, and murder and acts of violence committed in broad daylight, were daily occurrences."[49]

Hospital on Andreievsky Liman. Postcard.

So strong was Odessa's unsavory reputation that when Fedor Chalyapin, the famous basso, learned that Isaac Babel was from Odessa, he refused to entrust a valuable vase to him, even though Maxim Gorky had sent him a letter to convey the object to the author of *The Odessa Stories*.[50]

Another Jewish writer, Sholom Aleichem, created a character who visited Odessa. Menahem-Mendl is perhaps the mirror image of the rogues Benya Krik and Ostap Bender. He is an exuberant, naïve businessman, who in a letter to his wife raves, "I want you to know it is simply not in my power to describe the city of Odessa—how big and how beautiful it is—the people here, so wonderful and good hearted, and the terrific business one can do here."[51] These lines would not be so humorous if everyone, including the author, did not know how shady business could be in Odessa.

Menahem-Mendl thus was exceptionally optimistic at first about his business prospects in Odessa. But even he lost his money there. For most of its history Odessa has earned a reputation of defiance of Russian imperial and later Soviet law. As Paustovsky noted about the Civil War (1917–20), "even in those grim days racketeering flourished in Odessa. Even the most spineless caught the infection. . . . In time the rackets infiltrated even our literary and journalistic milieu."[52]

Tongue in cheek, Babel praises Romanians who came to Odessa after World War I:

> Nobody who loves Odessa can say a word against these Rumanians. They have brought life back to Odessa. They remind us of the days when the streets were full of trade, when we had Greeks trading in coffee and spices, German sausage makers, French book peddlers, and Englishmen in steamship offices. The Rumanians have opened restaurants, play music with cymbals, and fill taverns with their fast, foreign speech. They have sent us handsome officers with yellow boots and tall, elegant women with red lips. These people fit the style of our own.[53]

On the other hand, after World War II, during the Romanian occupation and administration of Odessa as part of Transnistria, crime and hooliganism reached new heights, matched perhaps only after 1991 when the nouveaux riches and mafiosi made their gaudy presence known.

Mention has been made of some of the famous writers of Odessa. Not only the physical beauty of the Southern Palmyra but also its lively population inspired a notable array of writers to record their memories, as we have seen, but at the same time to create works of imagination. While Alexander Kuprin was not a native, he visited the city often because he had many friends there. He incorporated scenes from the city in his stories such as "The Ballroom Piano Player," "My Flight," and "The Miraculous Doctor." He wrote about the seamier side of the port city's life. His *Yama*, or *The Pit*, shows the degradation of one of Odessa's

Fountain and front of telegraph building on Andreievsky Liman. Postcard, early 1910s.

brothels, while "Gambrinus" depicts some of the nightlife in the city's many cheap taverns. He was fascinated by

> all of these people—sailors of varied nationalities, fishermen, stokers, merry cabin-boys, port thieves, mechanics, workmen, boatmen, loaders, divers, smugglers—all young, healthy, and impregnated with the strong smell of the sea and fish, knew well what it was to endure, enjoyed the delight and the terror of everyday danger, valued, above anything else, courage, daring, the ring of strong slashing words, and when on shore, would give themselves up with savage delight to debauchery, drunkenness, and fighting.[54]

But Kuprin also noticed the brighter side of the city, "the dressed up, always holiday-like town, with its plateglass windows, its imposing monuments, its gleam of electric light, its asphalt pavements, its avenues of white acacias, its imposing policemen and all its surface of cleanliness and order."[55]

Odessa was up-to-date in many aspects, first with its horse-drawn trolleys, then electric trolleys installed as early as 1910. Olesha described seeing and riding the first trolley:

> I remember standing in a crowd on Grechsky Street and waiting with everyone else for the appearance of the trolley that had that day just gone into service for the first time. Everyone was certain that the trolley would be exceptionally fast—like lightning—and that you wouldn't even have time to consider whether or not you could run across the street in front of it. Yellow and red with a glass-enclosed platform in front, the trolley finally appeared. It was moving quite fast, although nowhere near the speed we had imagined. Greeted by our shouts, it passed in front of us, its platform crowded with people, including even a high-ranking priest, who sprinkled water in front of himself and the mayor of Odessa, Tomachev, who wore glasses and had a rust-colored moustache. A gentleman in a derby was at the controls, and everyone spoke his name. "Legoder!" He was the director of the Belgian firm that had built that first trolley line in Odessa.[56]

The London Hotel was (and is) an elegant place on Primorsky Boulevard. In 1904 it boasted electric lights, a salon, a reading room, baths, telephones, and a staff who could speak foreign languages. It was there that Kuprin first met the writer Anton Chekhov, whose roots were in nearby Taganrog on the Sea of Azov.

Yuri K. Olesha moved to Odessa as a child. His father, a Polish Catholic, was an excise officer in a vodka distillery. During the Civil War, Yuri's parents fled to Poland, but the young author remained in the city until his career as a journalist took him away eventually to Moscow, where he was friendly with other writers from Odessa—Katayev, Babel, Bagritsky, as well as Il'f and Petrov. Fascinated by painters, he saw the world with a painter's eye.[57] Olesha's most famous novel is *Envy* (1927), one that exhibited ambivalence toward the new Soviet values. He fell into disfavor with the regime; he returned to Odessa and during the Second World War went with the Odessa Film Studio to Turkmenistan. Olesha's memoirs reflect his fascination with film. His frequent references to Odessa, even when he lived in Moscow, confirm his statement that all that was lyrical and patriotic in his writing derived from his adopted city, Odessa, which he declared "was more closely tied to Europe than to Russia."[58]

Another translator confirmed the importance of Odessa in his writing, "nearly all of Olyesha's writings are colored by the sudden discovery, when he was four years old, of the bright radiance of Odessa high on its cliffs with the dark-blue sea beyond."[59] Olesha himself wrote, "It was a sky-blue Odessa day with something golden in it."[60] Konstantin Paustovsky, another Odessa writer and critic, and Olesha's friend ever since the Civil War, wrote after Olesha's death, "there was something of Beethoven in Yuri Olyesha, a great power, even in his voice. He saw with a wealth of magnificent details and he described them simply, accurately, and well."[61] More recently, a scholar wrote of Olesha's "comic genius, his skill as a storyteller, his slyly ironical and gamin slant on life (the birthright, apparently, of Odessa's writers.)"[62]

Like Olesha, who saw the world through a special carnavalesque lens, Mikhail Bakhtin "was born with a gift of laughter and a sense of the world as slightly mad."[63] Already fifteen years old when his family moved to Odessa, like many other writers he was affected by that multilingual and multinational city where he attended secondary school and began his university studies: "Odessa was an appropriate setting for a chapter in the life of a man who was to become the philosopher of heteroglossia and carnival. The same sense of fun and irreverence that gave birth to Babel's Rabelaisian gangster or to the tricks and deceptions of Ostap Bender, the picaro created by Il'f and Petrov, left its mark on Bakhtin."[64]

One of Olesha's friends was the poet Eduard Bagritsky, born Eduard Dzyubin to a middle-class Jewish family in Odessa in 1895. Olesha said in his memoirs, "As is well known, Bagritskii started out in Odessa. I was younger than he, yet not so much in years as they say, in the fact that he had already been published many times, while I had only been published once or twice. However, he liked me, and we were friends."[65] Bagritsky in turn had been powerfully influenced by the poet Vladimir Mayakovsky when Mayakovsky read his poems in Odessa at the Russian theater. In addition to Olesha, Bagritsky had as friends the writers Vera Inber and Valentin Katayev.[66]

Il'ya Il'f (Il'ya A. Fainzilberg) and Yevgeny Petrov (Yevgeny P. Katayev), both satirists from Odessa, drew upon their youth in Odessa. When living in Moscow they wrote two popular comic novels with Odessa settings thinly disguised: *Twelve Chairs* (1928) and *The Golden Calf* (1931), both of them mocking the vice of acquisitiveness, a trait perceived to be common to many Odessites. Il'f wrote a humorous piece in the magazine *Chudakh* in 1929, entitled "Trip to Odessa." In it he noted that before the revolution in Odessa there were only four monuments: to Richelieu, Vorontsov, Pushkin, and Catherine II. Then the number dwindled because the bronze autocrat was "overthrown." Tongue in cheek, he related that in the cellar of the Museum of History and Antiquities were scattered her extremities: her head, her skirt, and her bust, thus displaying her splendor to the occasional visitor. He went on to say (and the criticism is only implicit of the Bolshevik penchant for erecting monuments) that now there were no fewer than three hundred sculptures adorning the gardens, piazzas, boulevards, and streets: marble maidens, copper lions, nymphs, shepherds playing pipes, urns, and granite piglets. There were some piazzas, he claimed, where all of a sudden twenty or thirty such monuments could be seen.

Among those marble groves sprang up two lonely acacia trees. Graffiti decorated both the tree trunk and the waist of a marble maiden; he hinted that the statues were becoming eyesores. Without making an editorial comment, Il'f made it plain to the discerning reader that he did not think that Soviet architecture had improved the city. One wonders what tart remarks he might have made had he lived long enough to see the Soviet realist monument erected in 1977 to the mutinous Potemkin sailors, which took the place of the elaborate bronze statue of Catherine, the founder of Odessa.

Another writer of distinction who had ties to Odessa was Ivan Bunin, born in Moscow in 1870, a first-rate writer, and recipient of the Nobel Prize for Literature in 1933. Bunin was attracted to Odessa and lived there between 1918 and 1920—that is, before the Bolshevik takeover of the city. Thereafter, he left his beloved Russia forever. A friend of Anton Chekhov, he is said by the writer Leonid Andreyev to have been influenced by his experience of Odessa so that had he not lived there, his writing would have been of another character altogether. Valentin Katayev, a native Odessite and a novelist loyal to the Soviet regime, wrote that Bunin, who had inspired Katayev, was compromised by his antirevolutionary views, but that he never tried to hide them during the Civil War. Katayev took the young Olesha to meet Bunin, of whom Olesha said, "he is a pessimist, a spiteful, gloomy writer."[67]

Women writers also flourished in Odessa. Lesya Ukrainka (Larisa Petrovna Kosach), a Ukrainian writer, visited Odessa frequently between 1880 and 1909, even taking a cure at a local spa. She published her first volume of poetry, *On the Wings of Song*, in

Дерибасовская.   Одесса.
Rue de Ribas,   Odessa.

Deribasovskaya Street. Postcard, 1900s.

1904. Another poet, Vera Inber, born in 1890, became well known in her time. Her father owned a publishing company in Odessa, where she went to a girls' high school. While in her twenties she studied in Paris during the First World War and came under the influence of French and Russian Symbolism. She spent the Civil War years in Odessa. According to Paustovsky, Inber, who lived in a shady little street not far from him, was "a slight, frail woman." She spent many years in Western Europe, but returned to Leningrad before the Nazi invasion. She received a Stalin Prize for her account of the siege, *Almost Three Years*, a moving testimony to those awful times.

Perhaps the most famous poet born in Odessa was Anna Gorenko, who became a leading Acmeist. Indeed, she is probably the most famous of all Russian women poets. She took the name Akhmatova from her maternal Tatar great-grandmother. Her father was a maritime engineer and her aristocratic mother was a member of the revolutionary group The People's Will. Although she spent some time in Paris before the First World War, her name

is associated with Leningrad. She also spent time in the Black Sea area, in Evpatoriya and Lustdorf. When she was fifteen years old, she visited the cabin where she was born in Bolshoi Fontan, a suburb of Odessa. She said that someday there would be a plaque there, and indeed there now is one, put up by the city of Odessa. The city also changed the name of Ukraine Street to Akhmatova Street in 1987. Her fellow Odessa poet and prose writer Olesha said of her, "I consider her one of the most talented poets of the Russian constellation of the twentieth century."[68] Her beautiful lyrical cycle *Requiem* (1935–40), expressing her emotions at the time of the arrest of her son Lev, has universal appeal. She is also of cosmic importance since a crater on the love planet Venus bears her name. Called daughter of Odessa by virtue of her birth, she is claimed by all as their muse.

In the nineteenth century before railroads linked the area to the capital, Odessa seemed remote from the watchful eye of imperial surveillance. Somewhat peripheral to the solid Russian core of the empire, ethnic minorities who were on the fringe, both geographically and politically, found the liberal city suitable for launching secret liberation movements. There was also the possibility that if the authorities were in pursuit, one could make a hasty exit by sea. Thus Odessa was the site of the secret Greek society Philike Hetaria, which plotted the war for Greek independence from the Turkish Empire in 1821. Polish dissidents at the time of the 1861 uprising against Russian rule, together with their Ukrainian sympathizers, used the city as headquarters linking Kiev, Warsaw, London, Paris, and Geneva.

A Russian newspaper complained that Odessa was "the chief operational base of Polish activity and the international center for communications with all the revolutionary centers of Europe." Some Poles left Odessa to go to the barricades of Warsaw in the uprising of 1861; others came back to Odessa in exile, with their property given over to Russians.

Ukrainians formed their own nationalist societies; the most prominent were the Hromadas in mid-century and there was one in Odessa. Initially, they were loose associations of students and intellectuals interested in Ukrainian affairs, but then they took on a political slant, seeking reforms. Despite periods of repression, the Hromada in Odessa lasted until the Revolution of 1917. Another Ukrainian group, Prosvita, promoted the Ukrainian language by publishing literary and popular books and papers. It lasted for about a decade, but then it was suppressed so that only a cultural club for Ukrainians was allowed. The Bulgarian patriot Vasil Aprilov made Odessa a conspiratorial center for the raising of Bulgarian national consciousness through the Bulgarian Diocese. French Communards, defeated in Paris in 1871, also sought asylum in Odessa. Italian patriots manifested their enthusiasm for Garibaldi and his Red Shirts by putting in their shop windows signs with "Evviva Garibaldi." Even the great Garibaldi himself was a fisherman in the Black Sea area in his youth.

Like other ethnic groups, some Russians found the city to be a refuge, while others used it as a subterfuge for revolutionary activities. Before the emancipation of the serfs in 1861, many runaway serfs escaped to the port city. Odessa was considered by some to be a refuge, as were Kentucky and Massachusetts for American slaves. At the same time liberal Russians in Odessa were part of or sympathetic to the Decembrist revolt, a rebellion of officers in December 1825, who attempted to unseat Nicholas I. Some wanted his more liberal brother Konstantin to rule; others were fighting for a republic. With some justification, therefore, Tsar Nicholas I called Odessa a "nest of conspirators."

Students formed a secret Society of Good Goals, fourteen years to the day after the Decembrist revolt. More reformist than revolutionary, it inspired students at Moscow University to form an Odessa Circle that was concerned with social issues. A couple of decades later, workers in Odessa created the first politically active labor union, the South Union of Workers. Much celebrated

City Theater, rear view. Postcard.

by the Soviets, this group was soon disbanded by the police. Radicals showed more enthusiasm for the populist terrorist group "The People's Will." Not until 1900 was there a branch of the Social Democratic Workers' Party. This group included a large number of Jews, some of whom left the Jewish Bund that had formerly represented Jewish workers.

As a result of a downturn in the economy at the turn of the century, the number of socialists of all kinds grew in Odessa by 1900. To head them off the police allowed a charismatic Zionist, K. Shaevich, to form a police union. The workers did not realize that the police sponsored the union with the goal of limiting workers' demands to economic ones and to make sure political issues were not raised. The union enlisted thousands of workers who frequently went on strike, making economic demands. The police did not interfere with their efforts until 1903 at a time when strikes became more and more frequent; then in a sudden turnabout, Cossaks and soldiers brutally suppressed workers' meetings and put an end to strikes. The government deemed the experiment too dangerous. But such oppression only made the Social Democratic Party look more attractive.

Along with Poles, Ukrainians, Bulgarians, Greeks, and Italians, Jews also expressed nationalist sentiment, making Odessa one of the most important centers for Zionism in Russia. At first Jews left the traditional Pale of Settlement or the Galician city Brody for Odessa in order to make a better life for themselves. Because of their exposure to commerce, foreigners, foreign languages, and nontraditional schools, many Jews became assimilated into Odessa's society, departing from their traditional roots. That does not mean that Jews and gentiles mixed socially. The Zionist leader Vladimir Jabotinsky wrote in his diary that as a young boy growing up in the 1880s and 1890s in Odessa, he did not have a single close gentile friend, although his family was secular. Yet Jabotinsky would reminisce poetically about the joys of his boyhood spent in the light-hearted city by the sea where the inhabitants "babbled in a dozen languages."

For most Jews, business and living in the same neighborhoods brought them into frequent contact with gentiles. Haskalah, or the Jewish Enlightenment, found great support in Odessa more for practical than intellectual reasons. As Zipperstein noted, "Many Odessa Jews studied foreign languages, because knowledge of Italian, French, or German was deemed essential for participation in local economic life. Encouraged by the commercial opportunities open to Jews, many otherwise self-conscious traditionalists, unlike Orthodox Jews elsewhere in Russia, had their children study secular subjects to prepare for potentially lucrative commercial careers."[69]

In short, most of the Jews in Odessa were not rooted deeply in Orthodoxy. As Jabotinsky said of his youth, "Of the books we read, I do not recall one of Jewish content. The whole subject of Jews and Judaism just did not exist for us." He compared Jews in Odessa to those in Poland and Galicia: "In Odessa, I had not seen either the side-curls or the *kapota*, nor such wretched poverty. Nor had I seen grey-bearded, old and respected Jews, taking off their hats when they spoke to the gentile 'squire' in the street."[70]

Michael Stanislawski described the city as "a unique port city located geographically in Ukraine but populated by a mix of inhabitants: Russian bureaucrats, Greek and Italian merchants, and tens of thousands of Jews fleeing both the economic constraints and the religious and cultural conservatism of the Pale of Settlement. Odessa in Jabotinsky's youth was still a frontier town, a place noted for its irreverence and heterodoxy, its strange mixture of cosmopolitanism and seediness, Russianness and Europeanism."[71]

By the 1870s, however, economic opportunities shrank for Jews as well as for many others in the city. The grain trade that had sustained Odessa was slipping away to other Black Sea ports and worse yet, to the United States, India, and South America, giving less employment to stevedores, middlemen, exporters-importers, and factory workers. The result was not only pogroms, but also the radicalization of poor Jews along with poor Ukrainians and Russians. This radicalization of Jews manifested itself in their forming the Jewish Labor Bund and entering the ranks of the Social Democrats or the populists' terrorist groups.

Others decided it was useless to fight from within to better their condition; it was time to leave. The Odessa physician Lev Pinsker is typical of one who was much integrated into Odessa's cultural and intellectual life before the 1870s. But he had completely changed his mind about the future for Jews in Russia by 1882 (significantly a year after a violent pogrom in Odessa), when he published a pamphlet, *Autoemancipation*, proposing that Jews leave the Russian Empire. Moshe Lilienblum, once a firm supporter of Haskalah, eventually also became an ardent Zionist in Odessa, although earlier he had proposed that Jews should become agricultural colonists within the Russian Empire. Part of his disillusionment with the possibility of Jews finding happiness in Russia was based on his negative views of the city itself. He found life there too frivolous, and he resented *la jeunenesse dorée*, the obsession with commerce, money, and ease. In short, the materialism and superficiality of the city struck him as offensive. Only emigration to Palestine could solve the existential problems of life in Russia, especially in Odessa. For Lilienblum and for many other Jews, this commercial and luxury-loving city could be described as having the fires of hell burning around it, as a Jewish saying went.[72]

Other Jews loved the city for what it was. For example, Babel observed that Odessa was "the most charming city of the Russian Empire. If you think about it, it is a town where you can live free and easy. To a large extent it is because of [Jews] that Odessa has this light and easy atmosphere."[73] While some Jews like Lilienblum sought a Jewish homeland with higher values, others decided to leave because of the pogroms that darkened the pages of Odessa's history. Diversity characterized the city from its inception. One Swiss visitor wrote, "a Russian jostles against a Turk, a German against a Greek, an Englishman against an Armenian, a Frenchman against an Arab, an Italian against a Persian or a Bucharestian."[74] As in many cities in which diverse ethnic groups vie for space and employment, Odessa was never free from tension. "Jostling" erupted into violence from time to time as early as 1821, and then again in 1849, 1859, and in 1871. For the most part these frictions occurred between two immigrant groups—Greeks and Jews who competed for positions as grain merchants—but admittedly religious prejudice was also a factor.

The pogrom of 1871 occurred just when Jewish merchants were displacing Greeks in the grain trade. The Greek Orthodox church in Odessa was located in the middle of a Jewish neighborhood. Easter was always an occasion for much feasting, drinking, and revelry, breaking a forty-day fast. On this particular Easter, random shootings, rock throwing, and three days of looting of Jewish shops and homes accompanied the celebration. The

American consul in Odessa sent his report to Washington, D.C., saying "between the Jews and Greeks, therefore, there are constant jealousies and animosities, originating, no doubt, mostly from differences of race and religion, but also, perhaps, excited and encouraged from the collision of business interests."[75] The city voted to give compensation to Jews deprived of property.

Ten years later a more general pogrom in South Russia took on political overtones. Odessa was not the first to be affected, but in May 1881, riots and destruction of Jewish property ravaged the city for three days. It is suspected that a reactionary group, such as the "Holy Brotherhood," might have instigated the pogroms under the pretext that Jews were responsible for the assassination of Alexander II two months earlier. While the official explanation for the pogroms was that Jews were exploiting others in Odessa, most analysts spoke of economic rivalry for business in a city with declining opportunities and growing unemployment.

This pogrom resulted in the passing in 1882 of the May or Ignat'yev Laws, which legalized discrimination against Jews in Russia. They could no longer reside in villages, not even in the Pale of Settlement. They could not own land outside of cities—that is, engage in agriculture. They could not work on Sundays or other Christian holidays so that they might not have a competitive advantage over Christians. In general, these laws did not afford Jews the full protection of state law. On the contrary, they formalized the status of Jews as second-class subjects of the tsar. When Jews reacted to the pogrom of 1881 by creating a self-defense league (that also included Christian university students), they were accused of threatening the public order. The defense league was still intact in 1905, the year of the next pogrom in the city. Jabotinsky belonged to it. The myth was solidified therefore that somehow Jews were less loyal than others.

And it was this issue of patriotism that lay at the bottom of the next and most violent pogrom against Jews in Odessa, or at least it was the excuse adduced for persecution. The new wave of violence after twenty years of relative social peace came as the aftermath of the granting of a constitution by Nicholas II. This reluctant concession by the tsar was a result of massive strikes and revolutionary activity. Jews were accused of being in the forefront of those socialists, revolutionaries, and radicals who "forced" the tsar to give up some of his autocratic power. Of course many more gentiles than Jews were involved in revolutionary activity, but precisely because Jews were not the legal equals of others and were economic competitors, they provided a convenient target for blame.

View from Rishelyevskaya Street. Postcard.

Artisans were in general more radical than industrial workers and eagerly joined the Social Democratic Party, which had about a thousand adherents in Odessa by 1905. Since Odessa had a large number of artisans and most of them were Jews, there was the perception that revolutionaries in Odessa were Jews. By now economic tensions affected not only commercial enterprises but every business affiliated with the proper functioning of the port. The closing of the port during the war dried up credit, closed down the business of middlemen, and, most important, closed down factories and the work of those loading ships.

So by 1905 the city was in turmoil, especially after the arrival of the mutinous battleship *Potemkin*. Most of the strike activity and violence, such as the burning down of the port, was directed against the autocracy and capitalists. But it took a certain nasty turn after the October Manifesto, when the tsar was forced to make political concessions. Public disorders could easily turn from revolutionary goals into attacks on Jews.[76]

There was a perception that Jews were either very rich, in which case they were called exploiters, or very poor, in which case they were called an economic drain on the city. Olesha recalled some names in the first decade of the twentieth century: "The Odessa rich, I never saw any of them. I only heard their names: Brodsky, Gepner, Khari, Ashkinazi, Ptashnikov, Anatra. They were bankers, grain exporters—dark, sinister figures."[77] But the vast majority of Jews were very poor. Fierce competition among the poorest element of the population, the longshoremen, inflamed hatred between Russians and Ukrainians against Jews. In 1905 Jewish casualties amounted to 302 known dead including 55 from the self-defense force. Over 1,400 businesses were ruined. At this point many Jews decided that it was no longer possible "to live like God in Odessa." Thousands began their trek out of the city; between 1882 and 1908 a million Jews left Eastern Europe for the United States and elsewhere. Some of the Jews who remained did become socialists as a result of worsening economic conditions. For the most part they were Mensheviks, recruited from the economically and politically threatened artisans, merchants, and shopkeepers. Life went on in Odessa but under more unstable conditions.

Because of the relatively mild climate, as in many Mediterranean cities, so much of Odessa's vibrant life was led outdoors, either along its beaches, at the nearby dachas, in the parks, along Primorsky Boulevard, at the outdoor cafés and wine shops, and in the many interior city courtyards where people conversed, were observed, overheard, and intensely discussed. Business deals were concluded, robberies planned, and family quarrels were aired outdoors. The courtyard *(dvor)* afforded social space for entire families and groups of families, semi-secluded from the street. In the Moldavanka they also served as inns for travelers. Statues, wells, tables, benches, and grapevines decorated the cozy space that also served as a kind of political forum and newsroom. In some courtyards, especially in the Moldavanka, the *dvorniki* (superintendents or janitors) served as police informants. The Odessa-born writer, photographer, and printer Arkady Lvov published his novel *Dvor* in 1982; it takes place in Odessa during the Stalinist era, an indication that the courtyard was still the informal gathering place for political discussions as well as for the exchange of neighborhood gossip.

Outdoor cafés in Odessa also served as places for conversation, business deals, and sheer enjoyment of the long Odessa summers. Sholom Aleichem's character Menaham-Mendl gushes to his wife that he was privileged to sit in Café Fankoni, "side by side with all the big speculators at the white marble tables, and order a portion of ice cream, because in our Odessa, it is a custom that as soon as you sit down, up comes a man dressed in a coat with a tail and orders you to order ice cream."[78] Odessans did enjoy their food and drink. Almost all Odessans remember or still enjoy the delicious candy made by the Krakhmalnikov Brothers. Founded as a bakery in 1820 by Abram Wolf Krakhmalnik (1800–1883), the company was reorganized in 1893 by his sons Yakov (1860–?) and Lev (1864–1916) as a full confectionery. The chocolates, caramels, honey cakes, halva, and other treats were so fine that in the year 1904 alone the company won international gold medals in Paris, London, Moscow, and Rostov. When the Bolsheviks took over the factory, it employed five hundred persons; they renamed the plant the Rosa Luxemburg factory, which after 1991 became simply the Odessa Candy Company. It was one of the first candy factories to use candy

The New Stock Exchange, built in 1894–99, designed by Alexander Bernardazzi. Postcard, 1900s.

vending machines. Valetin Katayev, in his novel *Lonely White Sails*, has one character assure another that the gumdrop is a good one because it bore the Krakhmalnikov label. Mentioning the Rosa Luxemburg candy label in his novel *Envy*, which he wrote while living in Moscow, Olesha showed nostalgia for that particular candy.

Odessa's mild weather and spectacular light encouraged not only outdoor socialization but also painting. One of Russia's most popular and prolific painters was Ivan K. Aivazovsky. Born in Feodosiya in 1817, the son of an Armenian merchant, he painted over six thousand pictures of sailors and Odessa seascapes, including *The Black Sea* (1881). Odessa's mists filtered the light, especially in autumn, so that both sea and sunlight inspired painters. In his stories, Kuprin verbally painted the fog and mist that often covered the northern Black Sea. Paustovsky also described the atmosphere: "Odessa wrapped herself in mist, like the old women in their shawls. Sea fog lasted all through the autumn. I have been fond of misty days ever since—especially in autumn when the watery light is lemon-yellow like turning leaves."[79] Babel liked to describe the city in full light: "the sun hung from the sky like the pink tongue of a thirsty dog, the immense sea rolled far away to Peresip, and the masts of distant ships swayed on the emerald water of Odessa Bay."[80]

While scenery inspired some, music seems to have been one of the sources of inspiration for Wassily Kandinsky. Born in Moscow in 1866, he was taken to Odessa when he was five years old and stayed there until he was twenty. He became first an amateur cellist and pianist, and then a painter of abstract art. It is said that his early art mimics the abstract language of music he learned while living in Odessa. Although Kandinsky did not spend much of his adult life in Odessa, he visited his mother there from time to time. Leonid Pasternak, father of Boris the famous writer and Nobel Prize winner, was also an Odessa artist. A famous Jewish graphic artist was born in Odessa in 1893, Mikhail Dlugach. Like many of Odessa's writers, Dlugach moved to Moscow when it became the capital of the new Bolshevik state.[81]

Odessa had a passion for change, novelty, and experimentation. The good weather and beaches also encouraged sporting activities. As Babel noted of Odessa, "In the summer, the bronze, muscular bodies of youths who play sports glisten on beaches."[82] The writer Alexander Kuprin, "had he not become a writer, could certainly have been a champion boxer or wrestler. . . . Not satisfied with his prowess in these spheres, he threw himself into a host of others—fencing, skating, bicycling, horseriding, and even ballooning and aviation."[83]

Perhaps the personification of an athlete daredevil was Sergei Utochkin. Born in 1876 to a merchant family in Odessa, he was orphaned at an early age. His guardian gave him a bicycle, on which as a boy he loved riding around town. He soon became a champion bicyclist in Russia, winning an international prize in Lisbon before moving to faster vehicles—first the motorcycle, and then the automobile.

Isaac Babel celebrated Odessa's love affair with cars and Italian opera by depicting his most memorable character, the Odessan Jewish gangster Benya Krik, appearing at a funeral: "the red automobile came flying around the corner. It was honking *I Paglacci*."[84] And who can forget the con man Ostap Bender of the twenties portrayed in *The Little Golden Calf*, in his car bumping along the dusty roads of Odessa and environs?[85]

But Utochkin moved beyond automobile racing. He was also a runner, boxer, fencer, skater, yachtsman, and swimmer. Attracted to ballooning, he went to Egypt and flew over the pyramids and the Sahara desert. He made his reputation, however, as one of Russia's earliest aviators. By 1908, only five years after the Wright Brothers flew their first plane, he was a member of a select group belonging to the Emperor's All-Russian Air Club, Odessa branch, the only branch outside St. Petersburg. By April 1911, he was flying a French Farman IV biplane for the Odessa Naval Battalion. Earlier in 1910, he created a sensation in Baku, where he flew at an air show although he had never had flying lessons. So great was the interest in this spectacle that tickets cost over 60 rubles, the monthly wage of an oil worker. The audience gasped because it appeared that Utochkin would perish when his little plane went into a tailspin, but he managed to right it and land safely on the field. He had several other near misses in Ekaterinoslav and Rostov. Boasting that he would fly to Moscow in order to drink tea, he had a series of mishaps again en route with his plane. Lucky perhaps in flight but not in love, his beloved wife left him for a rich factory owner.

Not lucky for long, however, he injured himself severely during a difficult landing. At the hospital he was administered morphine; when he left, he became addicted to cocaine. He later was admitted to a psychiatric hospital in the capital, but was released in 1913 and went back to Odessa. When war broke out, he attempted to enlist in the air force but was refused. Even more humiliating, he was not allowed to work in an airplane construction factory. Returning to Petrograd, he was soon put back into the psychiatric hospital, where he died in 1916.

Babel wrote an epitaph of sorts: "I saw Utochkin, a *pur sang* Odessan, lighthearted and profound, reckless and thoughtful, elegant and gangly, brilliant and stuttering. He has been ruined by cocaine or morphine—ruined, word has it, since the day he fell out of an airplane somewhere in the marshes of Novgorod. Poor Utochkin, he has lost his mind. But of one thing I am certain: any day now the province of Novgorod will come crawling down to Odessa."[86] In his story "The Bicycle Chain," Olesha comments on Utochkin: "People regard him as a miracle. He was among the first to ride a bicycle, a motorcycle and an automobile, and one of the first to fly. He crashed on the Moscow-Petersburg flight and was gravely injured. They still laughed at him. He was the champion, and in Odessa he was regarded as a lunatic."[87]

In May 2001, Ukraine issued a special stamp in his honor. According to Kuprin, who first met the sportsman at Bolshoi Fontan on the seashore in the summer of 1904: "From that time on, I never could imagine Utochkin without Odessa, or Odessa without Utochkin." In September 2001, Odessa commemorated its athlete-pilot by placing on the steps of the Utochkina Cinema a statue of him with a paper plane in his hand as through he were about to launch it—a whimsical but perhaps fitting tribute to the daring pioneer aviator.

Writers were impressed by other sportsmen as well as Utochkin. Olesha played soccer in school, and was a great admirer of the game and of its stars as shown in his story, *Envy*.[88] Over the years, Odessa produced outstanding athletes including an Olympic champion in boating, Yuliya Ryabchinskaya, an Olympic champion in gymnastics, Margarita Nikolaevna, the gymnast Elena Vitrichenko, and the figure skaters Vyacheslav Zagorodnyuk, Victor Petrenko, and the "Swan of Odessa," Oksana Baiul. Lenny Krayzelburg, born in Odessa, won gold medals in swimming for the United States during the 2000 Olympics. As Jabotinsky wrote in his journal: "Odessa reared healthier types than most traditionally Jewish cities. Odessa did not have any tradition, but it was therefore not afraid of new forms of living and activity. It developed in us more temperament and less passion, more cynicism, but less bitterness. Were I asked, I would not choose to be born in any other city."[89]

Odessa seemed to foster characters of originality and a unique culture. As Rothstein so aptly explained: "thanks in large measure to the interaction of its populations of Russians, Jews, Ukrainians, Poles, Greeks, and others, Odessa produced its own dialect, its own music, its own humor, its own literature—and even its own version of gefilte fish."[90]

There have been many elegies written concerning the decline of Odessa at various stages of its history. During World War I, Babel wrote: "in Odessa there is a port, and in the port there are ships that have come from Newcastle, Cardiff, Marseilles, and Port Said; Negroes, Englishmen, Frenchmen, and Americans. Odessa had its moment in the sun, but now it is fading—a poetic, slow, lighthearted, helpless fading."[91] Jabotinsky, a native Odessite and Zionist, mused nostalgically: "No trace of that Odessa [of his youth at the turn-of-the-century] has existed for a long time, and there's no use hoping that I can ever return to it." And again he murmurs: "most likely, I shall never see Odessa again. Too bad, I love her."[92] Oleg Gubar, Odessa's contemporary historian, lamented the passing of old Odessa when "the sun shone brighter and the sky was bluer."[93] Others might even declare, "Odessa doesn't live here anymore," but Odessa lives in these pages of history and, more important, in the memories of present and past Odessites.

Brown University
June 2003

Opposite: Jewish klezmer musicians. Photograph, 1900s.

NOTES

Special thanks to Galya Diment, professor of Slavic Languages and Literatures, University of Washington, for help with this book.

1. Robert A. Rothstein, "How It Was Sung in Odessa: At the Intersection of Russian and Jewish Culture," *Slavic Review* 60, no. 4 (Winter 2001): 790.

2. Vladimir Jabotinsky, "Memoirs by My Typewriter," in *The Golden Tradition: Jewish Life and Thought in Eastern Europe*, ed. Lucy S. Dawidowicz (Syracuse: Syracuse University Press, 1996), p. 397.

3. Patricia Herlihy, *Odessa: A History, 1794–1914* (Cambridge, Mass.: Harvard University Press, 1986), p. 7.

4. General François De-Volant, *The Essay of My Service in Russia, 1787–1811* (Odessa, 1999).

5. Konstantin Paustovsky, *Story of a Life*, vol. 2, *Slow Approach of Thunder*, trans. Manya Harari and Michael Duncan (London: Harvill Press; New York: Pantheon, 1965), p. 217.

6. Isaac Babel, *The Complete Works of Isaac Babel*, ed. Nathalie Babel, trans. with notes by Peter Constantine (New York: Norton, 2002), p. 79.

7. Herlihy, *Odessa*, p. 232.

8. Michele de Ribas, *Saggio sulla Città di Odessa*, ed. Giovanna Moracci (Genoa, 1988).

9. Aleksandr De Ribas, *Staraia Odessa: Istoricheskie ocherki, vospominaniia* (Odessa, 1913).

10. Yuri Olesha, *No Day Without a Line* (Ann Arbor: Ardis, 1979), p. 142.

11. Patricia Herlihy, "Commerce and Architecture in Odessa in Late Imperial Russia," in *Commerce in Russian Urban Culture, 1861–1914*, ed. William Craft Brumfield, Boris V. Anan'ich, and Yuri A. Petrov (Washington, D.C., and Baltimore: Johns Hopkins University Press, 2001), pp. 180–94.

12. Herlihy, *Odessa*, p. 115.

13. Jabotinsky, "Memoirs by My Typewriter," p. 398.

Одесса. Старый базаръ.   Odessa. Le vieux bazar.

Staryi Bazaar.

14. Shmuel Katz, *Lone Wolf: A Biography of Vladimir (Ze'ev) Jabotinsky*, vol. 1 (New York: Barricade Books, 1996), p. 14.

15. Steven J. Zipperstein, *The Jews of Odessa: A Cultural History, 1794–1881* (Stanford: Stanford University Press, 1985), p. 66.

16. S. Y. Abramovitsh, *Tales of Mendele the Book Peddler*, ed. Dan Miron and Ken Frieden (New York: Schocken Books, 1996), p. 257.

17. Nicholas Luker, *Alexander Kuprin* (Boston: Twayne, 1987), p. 199.

18. Richard Taruskin, *Defining Russia Musically: Historical and Hermaneutical Essays* (Princeton: Princeton University Press, 1997), p. 188.

19. Zipperstein, *Jews in Odessa*, p. 30.

20. Zipperstein, *Jews in Odessa*, p. 66.

21. Babel, *Complete Works*, p. 628.

22. Ibid., p. 629.

23. Ibid., p. 701.

24. Rothstein, "How It Was Sung," p. 800.

25. S. Frederick Starr, *Red and Hot: The Fate of Jazz in the Soviet Union, 1917–1980* (New York: Oxford University Press, 1983), p. 144.

26. Rothstein, "How It Was Sung," p. 788.

27. Anatolii F. Kozak, *Odessa zdes' bol'she ne zhivet* (Samara, 1997), p. 139.

28. Richard Stites, *Russian Popular Culture: Entertainment and Society since 1900* (Cambridge: Cambridge University Press, 1992), p. 75.

29. Babel, *Complete Works*, p. 76.

30. Rothstein, "How It Was Sung," p. 789.

31. Ibid.

32. Ibid., p. 800.

33. Stites, *Russian Popular Culture*, pp. 21–22.

34. Paustovsky, *Story of a Life*, vol. 4, *Years of Hope*, p. 90.

35. Rothstein, "How It Was Sung," p. 800.

36. Stites, *Russian Popular Culture*, p. 48.

37. Paustovsky, *Story of a Life*, 2:93.

38. Olesha, *No Day Without a Line*, pp. 116–18.

39. Babel, *Complete Works*, p. 49.

40. Ibid., p. 75.

41. Rothstein, "How It Was Sung," pp. 783, 785.

42. Babel, *Complete Works*, p. 81.

43. Paustovsky, *Story of a Life*, vol. 3, *In That Dawn*, p. 205. See Boris Briker, "The Underworld of Benya Krik and I. Babel's *Odessa Stories*," *Canadian Slavonic Papers/Revue Canadienne des Slavistes* 36 (1994): 115–34.

44. Stites, *Russian Popular Culture*, p. 188.

45. Paustovsky, *Story of a Life*, 2:90.

46. Babel, *Complete Works*, p. 158.

47. Herlihy, *Odessa*, p. 282.

48. Roshanna P. Sylvester, "Crime, Masquerade, and Anxiety: The Public Creation of Middle Class Identity in Pre-Revolutionary Odessa, 1912–1916," Ph.D. dissertation, Yale University, 1998, pp. 237–240.

49. Herlihy, *Odessa*, p. 282.

50. Rothstein, "How It Was Sung," p. 791.

51. Sholom Aleichem, *The Adventures of Menahem-Mendl*, trans. Tamara Kahana (New York: Putnam, 1969), p. 17.

52. Paustovsky, *Story of a Life*, 4:10–11.

53. Babel, *Complete Works*, p. 82.

54. A. Kuprin, *Sasha*, trans. Douglas Ashby (London: S. Paul & Co., 1920), pp. 11–12.

55. Ibid., p. 9.

56. Olesha, *No Day Without a Line*, p. 88.

57. Rimgaila Salys, "Sausage Rococo: The Art of Tiepolo in Olesha's *Envy*," in *Olesha's Envy: A Critical Companion* (Evanston, Ill.: Northwestern University Press, 1999), p. 103.

58. Victor Peppard, *The Poetics of Yury Olesha* (Gainesville: University of Florida Press, 1989), p. 15.

59. Yuri Olyesha, *Love and Other Stories*, trans. with an introduction by Robert Payne (New York: Washington Square Press, 1967), p. ix.

60. Olesha, *No Day Without a Line*, p. 137.

61. Olyesha, *Love and Other Stories*, p. xxiii.

62. *The Portable Twentieth-Century Russian Reader*, ed. Clarence Brown (New York: Penguin, 1985), p. 250.

63. Katerina Clark and Michael Holmquist, *Mikhail Bakhtin* (Cambridge: Harvard University Press, 1984), p. 296.

64. Ibid., p. 27.

65. Olesha, *No Day Without a Line*, p. 146.

66. Maxim Shrayer, *Russian Poet/Soviet Jew: The Legacy of Eduard Bagritskii* (Lanham, Md.: Rowman and Littlefield, 2000), p. 97.

67. Olesha, *No Day Without a Line*, p. 251.

68. Olesha, *No Day Without a Line*, p. 170.

69. Zipperstein, *Jews of Odessa*, p. 21.

70. Katz, *Lone Wolf*, 1:26.

71. Michael Stanislawski, *Zionism and the Fin de Siècle: Cosmopolitanism and Nationalism from Nordau to Jabotinsky* (Berkeley: University of California Press, 2001), p. 126.

ПРИВѢТЪ

изъ ОДЕССЫ

Видъ на портъ отъ памятника Ришелье.

Souvenir postcard (detail), early 1910s.

72. Zipperstein, *Jews of Odessa*, p. 48.

73. Babel, *Complete Works*, pp. 14–15.

74. Herlihy, *Odessa*, p. 123.

75. Ibid., p. 302.

76. Robert Weinberg, *The Revolution of 1905 in Odessa: Blood on the Steps* (Bloomington: Indiana University Press, 1993).

77. Olesha, *No Day Without a Line*, p. 110.

78. Sholom Aleichem, *The Adventures of Menahem-Mendl*, p. 32.

79. Paustovsky, *Story of a Life*, 3:200.

80. Babel, *Complete Works*, p. 157.

81. Robert Weinberg, *Stalin's Forgotten Zion: Birobizhan and the Making of a Soviet Jewish Homeland* (Berkeley: University of California Press, 1998), p. 33.

82. Babel, *Complete Works*, p. 76.

83. Luker, *Alexander Kuprin*, p. 15.

84. Babel, *Complete Works*, p. 153.

85. Il'f and Petrov, *The Golden Calf*, trans. John H. C. Richardson (New York, 1965).

86. Babel, *Complete Works*, p. 76.

87. Olyesha, *Love and Other Stories*, pp. 210–11.

88. *Olesha's Envy*, p. 5.

89. Jabotinsky, "Memoirs by My Typewriter," p. 399.

90. Rothstein. "How It Was Sung," pp. 800–801. Babel proclaimed that Odessa-style gefilte fish with horseradish was "a dish worth embracing Judaism for" (*Complete Works*, p. 48).

91. Babel, *Complete Works*, p. 7.

92. Stanislawski, *Zionism*, pp. 237 and 235.

93. Oleg Gubar, *100 voprosov za Odessu* (Odessa, 1994), p. 2. He wittily described his book as a "short course" on Odessa's history for "all-class reading."

Одесса. Городской театръ.

City Theater. Postcards, early twentieth century.

ОДЕССА. Люстдорфъ, Ст: Электрическаго Трамвая.
ODESSA. Loustdorff-Station du Tramway éléctrique.

Съ Рождество
Христовымъ

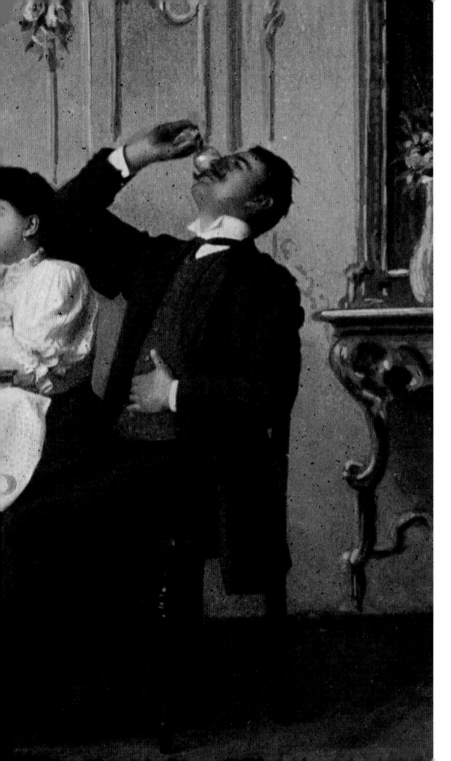

Одесса. — Николаевскій Бульваръ.
Odessa. — Boulevard de Nicolas.

Одесса, Видъ на Строгановскій мостъ
Odessa, Pont Stroganov

Odessa Public Library, built in 1907.

Одесса.
Видъ на городъ съ Николаевско-Херсонской
пристани.
Odessa.
Aspect de la ville, vue de l'embarcadère de
Nikolayeff Kherson.

Одесса.　　Большой фонтанъ.　　Старый маякъ.

Grande Fontaine.　Les rives d'or.

Одесса. Карантинная Гавань.

Одесса. Берегъ Дача „Отрады".

Одесса. Малый Фонтанъ.

ОДЕССА. Ланжеронъ. — ODESSA. Langéron.

Одесса. Воронцовскій маякъ.

Daily Life in Odessa

Oleg Gubar & Alexander Rozenboim

Translated by Antonina W. Bouis

Left and above (detail): The citizenry celebrating Easter Sunday. Postcard, early twentieth century.

Odessa's personality, humor, and love of life are legendary, though its situation on the map of Europe is rather modest. Russian settlers on this enormous frontier encountered the same difficulties their distant transoceanic brethren faced on the prairies of the American Wild West—no reliable water supply in drought conditions, a lack of natural fuel and appropriate construction materials, and unfavorable engineering and geological conditions. There were no safe harbors. The environment was hostile and fraught with military dangers and deadly epidemics.

Odessa was founded on a settled point that had served for centuries as a trade entrance into the northern Black Sea. At the turn of fifth century B.C. there were Greek trading posts, including one called Edesa/Ordes a few dozen kilometers northeast of the present city. Pliny the Elder, Flavius Arrianus, and Claudius Ptolemy mention the town.

These entrepôts later became Roman, Byzantine, medieval Italian, Tatar, Polish, and Turkish. Testament to Odessa's early trading prowess can be seen in the thirty-two vessels of all periods and nations that have been found by hydrographers at various depths, including medieval galleys, paddle boats, and military ships and submarines from the two world wars. Exotic anchors of various sizes are periodically found not only within the waters of Odessa Bay but also in the Kuyalnitsky and Khadzhibeisky *limans* [from the Greek *limen*, i.e., bay]. In the Middle Ages, the limans were connected to the sea, and Genoese and Venetian sailors took shelter there in their galleys and ships. On ancient Italian charts and maps, this anchorage—the predecessor of Odessa—is called Ginestra. Odessa's other precursors included Harbor of the Istrains or Harbor of the Asiaks, Kachibei, Khadzhibei, and finally Eni-Dunya, the last Turkish garrison, erected in 1765 from French blueprints, and taken by Russian troops under the command of Major General De Ribas on 14 September 1789, killing more than two hundred men in the battle and taking prisoners that included the fort's commandant, Pasha Ahmet, twelve officers, and sixty-six soldiers.

Osip Mikhailovich Deribas (Don Joseph de Ribas) is a legendary figure in the history of Odessa. His father was Spanish (de Rivas) and his mother Irish (or, according to some, French). De Ribas served in the Neapolitan Army, from which he transferred to the Russian Navy through the patronage of Count Alexis Orlov, one of Empress Catherine the Great's favorites. He was then only twenty-five and dreamed of doing noble deeds in the style of medieval knights. Russia gave him the opportunity: De Ribas fought for her on land and sea—in infantry, cavalry, rowed flotilla, and canon ship. His troops stormed several Turkish fortresses, including Ismail, an exploit Byron celebrated in *Don Juan*.

Extraordinary rumors and gossip swirled around De Ribas, and the powers-that-be intrigued against him. They said, not

Deribasovskaya Street. Postcard, early twentieth century.

without foundation, that he had been the chief plotter in the kidnapping of the adventuress "Princess Tarakanova," a pretender to the Russian throne. He was accused of bribery, embezzlement, being a shill for cheating at cards, and even bigamy. De Ribas was indeed a man of action—daring and impatient—and he did have an illegitimate son, did play cards professionally, and was not always rational in his use of money. But he was no bigamist, card sharp, or bribe taker. He had two daughters—Catherine and Sophia—both godchildren of Empress Catherine II.

In a royal note to De Ribas dated 27 May 1794, the empress instructed him to begin building a significant military and commercial port at the village of Khadzhibei. However, the real first day of Odessa's life is considered to be 22 August (2 September New Style) 1794, the day that the first piles were driven for the piers, a symbolic furrow was drawn on city land, the lots to be given to the first settlers for construction were plotted, and the first churches were started. At the intersection of the future

Lanzheronovskaya and Rishelyevskaya streets, the very heart of Odessa, the foundation was laid for the first official residence, belonging to the chief military leader of the empire's southwest region, Prince G. S. Volkonsky. The ceremony consisted of the participants—apparently, De Ribas, Volkonsky, and the actual director of the construction of the city and port, the military engineer F. P. De Voland—smashing a bottle of fine wine and several delicate crystal goblets against the stones. Along with the ritual coin bearing the empress's monogram, fragments of the glasses, the crystal tray, the bottle, and even the cork were found by archeologists in the foundation trench, under the base of the masonry wall.

Odessa's historical center lies on a high rolling plateau, with sea cliffs reaching 45–48 meters, and divided by three *balki* (broad ancient peat-filled ravines)—the Karantinny, Voenny, and Vodyannoi (Quarantine, Military, and Water)—which have long served as transportation arteries between the city and the port. As it grew, the city moved beyond the *balki* and expanded in an arc around the Odessa Bay, from Point Lanzheron to Point Odessky-Severny, and to the southeast to the former German colony of Lustdorf (today called Chernomorka). Former suburbs eventually found themselves within the city limits: for example, Moldavanka (originally settled by people from Walachia and Moldavia), Maly, Sredny, and Bolshoi Fontany (Small, Medium, and Big Fountains: the word *fontan* was used for geysers); Blizhnie (near) and Dalnie (far) Melnitsy (mills); Slobodka-Romanovka (from the Russian *sloboda*, large village or suburb); Bugaevka (from the Ukrainian *bugai*, bull); and Peresyp (from the Slavic word for sifting), which is a sand and shell strip separating two saltwater reservoirs—Khadzhibeisky and Kuyalnitsky bays—from Odessa Bay; it borders the port and has became a major industrial center. In general, all the Black Sea bays are former river valleys that "drowned" when the sea moved onto dry land.

Grand Fontaine. Postcard, early 1900s.

Odessa was built according to the general plan developed by the talented military engineer of Dutch extraction—Franz De Voland. The plan called for a system of straight, perpendicular streets, whose direction was determined by the orientation of the deep ravines dividing the Odessa plateau. Thus the *balki* became the natural slopes from the high shore to the port. To the west of the rectangle of streets another network of blocks was planned at an angle of 45 degrees from the first. This way all the streets eventually led to the sea. These two major sectors were called Voenny (Military) and Grechesky (Greek). With only minor alterations De Voland's plan was used to create what is today's historical center of Odessa.

The city's galloping commercial growth was due to a fortunate combination of historical, geographic, and economic circumstances. The partition of Poland in 1793 opened up the road south for many of its agrarian regions. War-torn Europe acutely needed agricultural products. Turkey had lost its preeminence as a

Clockwise from top left: Portrait of Admiral Osip Mikhailovich Deribas (Joseph de Ribas), I. B. Lampey the Elder, 1798; Parkhet, *The Conquest of Khadzhibei Fortress,* 1950s; (Russian troops under Major General De Ribas storming Eni-Dunya Castle, 14 September 1789); Count Louis Alexandre de Langeron (1763–1831), 1820s. Lithograph; Mercury, patron of trade, on the statue of the Duc de Richelieu, 1898; Fragment of the monument to Catherine II dismantled by the Bolsheviks.

Ки. Г. А. Потемкинъ.
трополитъ Гавріилъ.
Графъ И. В. Гудовичъ.
Абб. Николь.

Императрица Екатерина II.
Императоръ Александръ I.
Ки. А. В. Суворовъ.

Императоръ Павелъ.
Адмир. І. де-Рибасъ.

Ки. П. А. Зубовъ,
Арх. Гавріилъ,
Герцогъ де-Ришельё,
А. Ѳ. Ланжеронъ,

Первоначальныя времена Одессы.

Clockwise from left: Allegorical painting circulated for Odessa's centenary, 1894, celebrating historical figures involved in the founding and development of Odessa: Empress Catherine II, Prince G. A. Potemkin-Tavrichesky, Prince P. A. Zubov, Metropolitan Gavriil and Archbishop Gavriil, the Emperors Paul I and Alexander I, Count I. B. Gudovich, Prince A. V. Suvorov, Admiral De Ribas, Duc de Richelieu, Abbot Nikol (the first director of the Richelieu Lycee), Count de Langeron, a symbolic depiction of Mother Russia with Infant Odessa on her lap, surrounded by "children of various nations": an Italian girl with a violin, a German girl with a guitar, a Polish girl with a lute, an Albanian girl with a triangle, a Ukrainian girl with a *domra*, and a Russian boy with a flute; "The Ritual of the Establishment of Odessa," exhibit at Odessa State Historical Regional Studies Museum; Souvenir postcard, early 1900s; The house of mill owner Inber. Postcard, early 1900s.

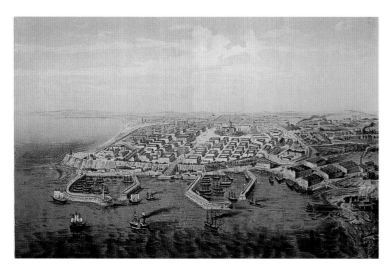

Bird's-eye view of the city, harbor, and fortifications, 1855. Lithograph, artist unknown.

Mediterranean power. The city was being built between the deltas of a network of major water arteries: on one side the Dniepr and Yuzhny Bug and on the other the Dniestr and Danube. The waters of Odessa Bay froze only occasionally and briefly. All that was needed was a port. In the second year of its existence, Odessa had the first docks, slipways, wharves, embankments, barracks for 16,000 soldiers and sailors, and warehouses for grain and salt. Skippers from all over the Mediterranean quickly came to transport the grain, and maritime offices from every European country got involved. The port of Odessa was defended by five batteries and the new fortress at the top of Point Lanzheron by eighty-eight guns.

There was a "dynasty" of Vorontsov lights and lighthouses, replaced one after the other throughout the history of the Odessa port. The last Vorontsov lighthouse was built in 1888. The graceful 17-meter cast-iron tower that narrowed toward the top was crowned with Frenel system lighting apparatus imported from Paris. The white tower, life rings, surrounding chains, gleaming brass bell, steep stone steps leading to the water, and the red light keeping watch at night constituted for many people Odessa's proud symbol. The lighthouse was blown up in the summer of 1941 so that the Germans could not use it as orientation in shelling the city.

Another landmark of the port was the overpass built in 1872 for the railroad. For its time, the bypass was a masterful feat of engineering, a four-kilometer road spanning the entire port. Thanks to the height of the railroad track (six meters above the berths), the grain moved by gravity through the pipes and chutes into the holds of ships. The bypass, made of solid oak beams, burned in a fire at the port in 1905 during the mutiny on the battleship *Potemkin*, but it was restored. In 1919 during a terrible Civil War fuel shortage in Odessa, it was taken apart piece by piece for firewood.

The arcade wall and tower is the remaining fragment of the Quarantine, built in the early nineteenth century, which was considered a model throughout Europe. The word *quarantine* comes from the French *quarante*, or "forty," referring to the number of days of confined observation required during threats of epidemic. Such threats were frequent in Odessa: in 1812 the plague took the lives of 2,650 citizens; four of the city's five doctors were infected by their patients and died. Two hundred Odessites died of the plague in 1829, 731 of cholera in 1831, 108 of plague in 1837, and 1,861 of cholera in 1848.

Quarantine was strict. Everyone entering Odessa during a dangerous period had to spend two weeks in quarantine. Personnel working in the Quarantine wore special uniforms and red markings so that no one dared touch them. Watchmen on the walls and towers were armed and prepared to shoot anyone who dared escape their surveillance.

There was never a more revered figure in Odessa than the Duc de Richelieu. He transformed it into a European city and a major

Port of Odessa and Vorontsov Palace, 1830s. Lithograph.

transit point in the trade between East and West. He spurred
grain exports by bringing in agrarian colonists from Germany,
Switzerland, France, and other countries; he freed Odessa from
exorbitant taxes, and proposed a *porto-franco* (free port). It was
Richelieu who made sure that the grain trade between Russia and
Turkey continued even when the countries were at war. Risking
his life, he entered plague-ridden houses to cheer up the citizens
and share his last piece of bread. The Duc gave all his money to
create the largest educational institution in the south of Russia—
the lycée. He also built the City Theater, where the best opera
troupes of the empire performed.

For eleven years (1803–14), first as mayor of Odessa and then
governor-general of the entire New Russia region, the Duc lived
in a decrepit one-story house, "furnished" with stools and trestle
beds that had lost their shellac. He did all his own clerical work,
answering every letter, usually in the language in which it was
written. He ate modestly. He paid the salaries of his small office
staff. Every day he made the rounds of the city and outlying
regions, chatting with merchants, contractors, army men, doctors,
guests of the city, foreign diplomats, and ordinary folk. He attended all the public and private balls. Seriously concerned with
the greening of the arid territory (old Khadzhibei had only two
or three trees), Richelieu imported saplings from Europe and per-
sonally inspected every new tree, watering them himself.

Richelieu came from an ancient aristocratic line that included
Louis XIII's famous cardinal, but his impressive pedigree did not
keep him from being the most human of Odessa's administrators.
In fact, France may not have known a better foreign minister than
Richelieu; it was this post he took up on his return to his homeland in 1814 from Odessa. When he died in 1822, Emperor Alexander I told the French ambassador, "I mourn the Duc de Richelieu
as the only friend who told me the truth. He was the model of
honesty and truthfulness."

One of Richelieu's greatest achievements was his sponsorship
of the City Theater, completed in 1809, designed by Thomas de
Thomon. The theater played a more important role in Odessa
than in any other Russian city. Like the thermal baths of Rome,
it served as a social gathering place for discussion of commerce,
politics, and other news, display of the latest fashions, and so on,
presupposing equality of all its participants. The theater held a
similar place in Italy in the seventeenth and eighteenth centuries.
As part of the orbit of Mediterranean trade, Odessa borrowed
many elements of life style from Italy, France, and the Levant.

Thus, Italian opera became a significant phenomenon in the
city's cultural life. Each season the troupe obtained new members
and new works from Italy. Many operas had their Russian pre-
mieres in Odessa rather than St. Petersburg or Moscow, especially
works by Rossini (*Cinderella, The Barber of Seville, An Italian in
Algiers, Semiramide, William Tell, The Thieving Magpie*, and
Mathilde di Charban). The great Catalani and Moriconi per-

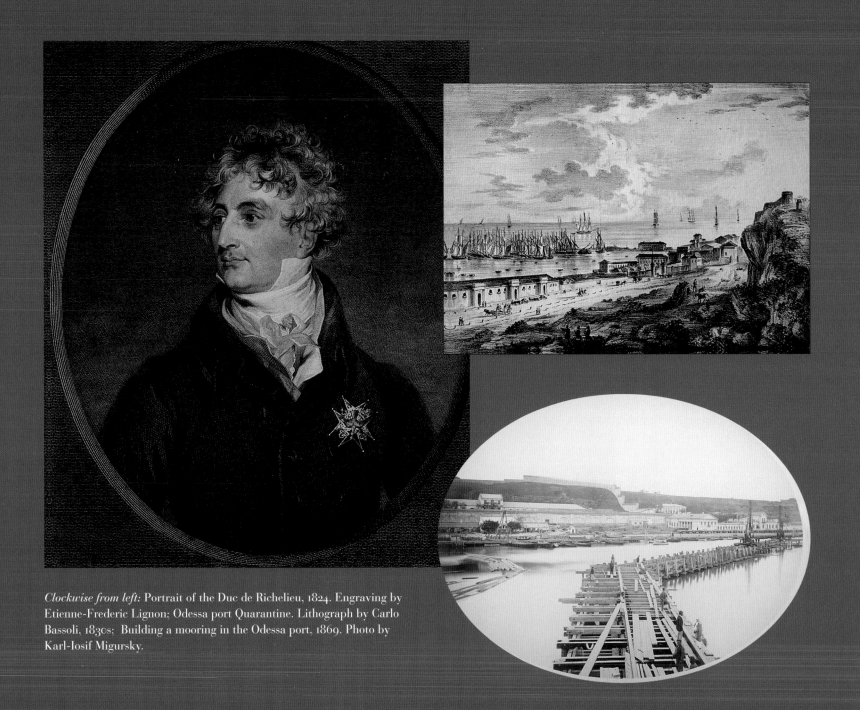

Clockwise from left: Portrait of the Duc de Richelieu, 1824. Engraving by Etienne-Frederic Lignon; Odessa port Quarantine. Lithograph by Carlo Bassoli, 1830s; Building a mooring in the Odessa port, 1869. Photo by Karl-Iosif Migursky.

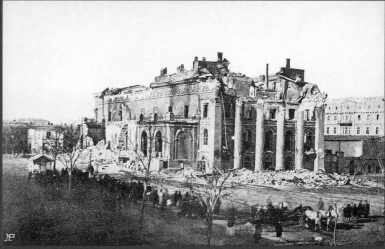

Clockwise from top left: The Vorontsov Lighthouse, 1900; The City Theater after the fire of January 1873. Photo by Karl-Iosif Migursky. OGNB: The Richelieu Lycée in the 1830s. Lithograph; Statue of the Duc de Richelieu. Postcard, 1900s.

formed on the Odessa stage. Over the years, the theater offered its stage to such outstanding composers as Liszt, Mussorgsky, Tchaikovsky, Rimsky-Korsakov, Glazunov, Ippolitov-Ivanov, Rachmaninoff, and Rubinstein and such vocalists as Chalyapin, Sobinov, Ruffo, and Nezhdanova. A great fan of Italian opera, Alexander Pushkin left vivid descriptions of the theater and its patrons. Another important legacy is the Richelieu Lycée, which became one of the largest and most respected educational institutions in southern Russia in the first half of the nineteenth century. In 1817, it was created on the base of the Noble Educational Institute, founded by Richelieu in June 1805, and financed by him and by funds from Odessa's grain export trade. This was the second lycée in Russia after the one near St. Petersburg in Tsarskoe Selo, where the sons of prominent aristocratic families studied. The lycée diploma was equivalent to a university degree. It was a closed institution of the military type. The ten-year course emphasized European and ancient languages, rhetoric, philosophy, history, geography, physics, and mathematics, fortifications, artillery science, geodesy—everything required of a future officer. They also studied drawing, dancing, singing, fencing, and religion. In 1837 the Richelieu Lycée was officially made a higher education institution and in 1865 it was restructured into the Imperial New Russia University.

Richelieu's successor, Louis Alexandre, Comte de Langeron (1763–1831), was governor of Odessa, military governor of Kherson, and head of the civil part of all of the New Russia region from 1815 to 1822. It was in his regime that the idea for a porto-franco was realized, the Richelieu Lycée was established, the ground broken for the Botanical Gardens, and the city's first newspaper began publication in French. As a beardless youth, Langeron fought with the French expeditionary corps on the American continent. With the Russian Army he fought against the Swedes and in two campaigns against the Turks. Like Richelieu he took part in the storming of the mighty Turkish citadel Ismail, and fought against the French at Austerlitz. Langeron's honesty and directness caused him a lot of trouble. A brave soldier, he did not understand social diplomacy and could not deal with court intrigues. The noble and democratic Langeron is commemorated in one of Odessa's main streets, Lanzheronovskaya, where the count's house still stands.

Odessa's multinational, cosmopolitan character derives from Russian state policy in the late eighteenth and early nineteenth centuries, which sent significant human and material resources to the Black Sea to domesticate the huge territory annexed after wars with the Ottoman Empire. The democratic principles of registering as urban citizens, tax breaks for the bourgeoisie and merchants for several decades, free homesteading, loans, and equality of foreign and Russian subjects opened up Odessa to businessmen, craftsmen, and farmers of all nations. In the first half of the nineteenth century, almost half of the population was made up of ethnic foreigners, either citizens of Russia or other nations. By comparison, the number of foreigners in St. Petersburg was no more than 7.5 percent, and less than 1 percent in Voronezh and Kharkov.

From its founding, the city's Greek community made up about 10 percent of the population. Almost all foreign trade, especially grain, was concentrated in Greek hands (Rodokanaki, Papudov, Marazli senior, Ralli) until the second half of the nineteenth century, when the Jewish business community gained preeminence. The Greeks also dealt in retail trade—meat, fish, and groceries. Like the Bulgarians, the Greeks were brilliant gardeners, and they were reportedly the most skilled fishermen and sailors. They did little in crafts, but there were shoemakers, bakers, and manufacturers of oriental sweets (halvah, rakhat-lukum) and tobacco products. Greek wine merchants played a significant role.

At the time Admiral De Ribas took Khadzhibei, there were six Jews living there. One hundred years later, they numbered 138,000,

View of Odessa port. Photograph, late nineteenth century.

the largest Jewish population in Europe. It grew through immigration from small Jewish villages and agricultural colonies of Russia and particularly from the Austrian province of Galicia and its city, Brody, which was celebrated for its famous rabbis and Jewish wise men. Galician, or as they were called in Odessa, Brodsky Jews took Russian citizenship and became citizens of Odessa; only their German-sounding names suggested that they had been foreigners. The leadership of the Odessa Jewish community was quickly taken by the Brodsky Jews, who tended to be richer, better educated, and more reform-minded than other immigrant groups. Their descendants included the writer Isaac Babel, the virtuoso violinist Mischa Elman, and Leonid Pasternak—father of poet Boris Pasternak. Russian Jews tended to have surnames formed from their original villages: Zhvanetsky from the village of Zhvanets, Bershadsky from Bershadi, Medzhibovsky from Medzhibozh, a renowned center of Hassidism.

In the first few decades of the nineteenth century thousands of Jews moved to Odessa—tailors, merchants, teachers, shop owners, shoemakers, watchmakers, synagogue servants, jewelers, bookbinders, cemetery guards, owners of money changing offices, upholsterers, and people without professions hoping to find their luck in the thriving young city. Unlike many other cities, there was no Jewish quarter. Jews lived all over Odessa, but there were areas of greater density: the suburb of Moldavanka; the streets called Evreiskaya (Jewish), Bazarnaya (Bazaar), and Staroreznichnaya (Old Butcher), where there were many butchers who handled fowl in accordance with Jewish religious law; and Malaya Arnautskaya (Small Arnaut), where Jews lived side by side with Albanians, who baked bread and were called Arnauts.

Accustomed to communal life in the small villages, the new Jewish Odessites created a community; opened a synagogue, a butcher shop, school, hospital, public baths, and cemetery; organized the first philanthropic societies; and in 1795 began keeping the *pinchas*, a kind of chronicle of the community. In its pages,

Odessa under Langeron. Engraving, 1823.

we find many interesting events: Meir Elmanovich was elected a member of the city magistrate's office, Khaika Tsolfovichev complained about her husband's improper behavior during his business trips away from Odessa, the Natanzon brothers opened a store in the house of Countess Langeron on Lanzheronovskaya Street, and some Jewish youths, crazed by the liberties of the local mores, beat up a rabbi. Odessa's remoteness from the traditional Jewish religious centers, the city's multinational character, the opportunities for broad and successful participation in trading operations and banking all contributed to a gradual weakening in the role of religion and ritual in the life of local Jews.

Although the French, Swiss, British, and Italians did not form a large percentage of the population, they had a strong cultural influence. The Italian influence is perhaps the most obvious. In the first decades of the nineteenth century, Italian was taught in all the Odessa schools. Signs with names of streets, stores, and cafes were written in Russian and Italian. The Italian casino of Theater Square was the traditional meeting place of exporters. Italian navigators had the priority in creating sea charts guaranteeing the safety of sea trading. Memoirs show that even the coachmen had a vast knowledge of popular Italian opera arias, and that the melodies of Rossini and Cimarosa could be heard coming from the mouths of ordinary men on the street. The Italians also traded in wines, imported marble, olive oil, dried fruit, and other products. They worked as brokers at the stock exchange. In the first half of the nineteenth century they baked bread and manufactured macaroni, galettes, sausages, and confectionery. Most of the revered architects of Odessa were Italian: the Frapolli brothers, Boffo, Toricelli, Morandi, and Bernardazzi. The same holds for sculptors and marble workers: Iorini and Menzione. Italians taught music and singing and there were many Italian painters in Odessa.

Apart from their dominance of city administration through Richelieu and Langeron, the French made invaluable contributions to the organization of the commercial infrastructure: the

Bazaar at Moldavanka, early twentieth century.

first bank (Fournier et Jaume), the first commercial court of the Russian Empire (Count Saint-Pris), the first shipping and insurance offices, and the first financial newspaper (Jean Davallon), as well as the creation of the first processing plants. Odessa's French colony grew grapes and orchards and raised sheep and silkworms. The French were the city's best couturiers, coiffeurs, restaurant owners, chefs, and furniture makers. They also started the production of stearine candles, soaps, glue, powders, and so on. The Swiss in Odessa were primarily of French extraction. The Swiss established vineyards with European varieties of grapes in their colony called Chabeau to the southwest of the city. Many people from the French cantons took positions as governesses, teachers, and maids in Odessa homes.

There were not many British in Odessa but they played an important role in trade: in the first decades of the nineteenth century England supplied all of southern Russia with coal and exported Russian goods. The German community had an almost complete range of craftsmen: smiths, carpenters, coach builders, cabinetmakers, gunsmiths, watchmakers, bakers, sausage makers, printers, and others. There were doctors and pharmacists. There were factory owners as well as middle school and university teachers. The German colonists were responsible for the spread of agriculture throughout the Black Sea region, for creating the optimal system of land use, and for introducing agricultural technology. Among the German Odessites were quite a few who started out in neighboring agricultural colonies and then made brilliant careers as major factory owners. Among them we must mention the famous Faltz-Fein family, proprietors of the largest fish cannery in the region. The best agricultural tools made in the South were produced by the former colonist Johann Hohn, who founded an enormous factory in Odessa. The Trading House of Bellino-Fenderikh, known well beyond Odessa, manufactured agricultural and other tools.

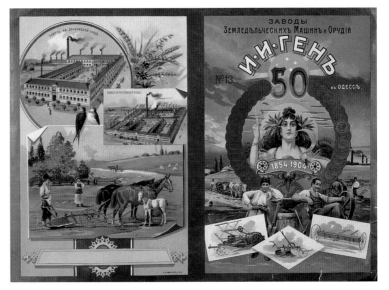

Some of the world's largest manufacturers of agricultural equipment had stores and warehouses in Odessa—for example, Hugo Grunert, McCormick, and Osborne. In the first stage of the city's existence, quite a few Polish landowning aristocrats settled there and dealt in grain export. There were Polish doctors, lawyers, notaries, pharmacists, and craftsmen. Many Poles worked in the service sector; they were the overwhelming majority of household servants.

In the early nineteenth century, Germans settled in two areas called Upper and Lower colonies. The Upper Colony was grouped around Nemetskaya (German) Street, later named Yamskaya and Novoselskaya. Branching off from it were streets named for the professions of the settlers: Kuznechnaya (Smith) and Degtyarnaya (Pitch) as well as Luteransky Alley, leading to the church. The Lower Colony developed Remeslyannaya (Crafts) Street and Karetny (Coach) Alley. The Greek diaspora was established around the Greek Bazaar. There also lay Grecheskaya (Greek) Street and Krasny Alley, named for the Krasny rows of the Greek Bazaar. In Russian, *krasny*, literally "red," means beautiful and in this case "quality" goods. The magnificent Greek Church of the Holy Trinity was situated a few blocks from there.

Bolshaya and Malaya Arnautskaya streets recalled the presence of Albanians (Arnauts), who served in the Russian navy and

Opposite, clockwise from left: Advertisement for Faltz-Fein, the largest fish cannery in the region; Advertisement for agricultural tools made by the former colonist Johann Hohn, who founded an enormous factory in Odessa.; The Trading House of Bellino-Fenderikh, known well beyond Odessa, manufactured agricultural and other tools. *Right and following pages:* Some of the world's largest manufacturers of agricultural equipment had stores and warehouses in Odessa—including Hugo Grunert, McCormick, and Osborne.

МАШИНЫ

Мак КОРМИКА

СКЛАДЪ **И. МАШЕВСКАГО** въ ОДЕССѢ.

ДОЗВОЛЕНО ЦЕНЗУРОЮ ОДЕССА. 16ГО МАРТА 1894 Г. ХРОМОЛИТОГРАФІЯ В. ТИЛЬ и Кⁿ ОДЕССА.

fought in numerous battles in the Mediterranean. There are other "ethnic" names in Odessa—for example, streets called Polskaya, Bolgarskaya, Malorossiiskaya, and Evreiskaya, and Frantsuzsky Boulevard. Only Italyanskaya Street did not last and was renamed Pushkinskaya long before the revolution.

Old Odessa had dozens of Russian Orthodox, Catholic, evangelical, Lutheran, reform, and Anglican churches; three large and many small synagogues; a Karaite kenass; and a Muslim mosque. Promoting freedom of religion, the first administrators of Odessa attended churches of various denominations. All religions had schools for clergy, which were open not only to people of their own faith but to anyone interested.

The best example of Odessa's cosmopolitanism is the ethnic representation in the city government, the Duma. Before 1863 the Odessa Duma was not absolutely democratic with members from every stratum, but even then there were numerous Jewish, Greek, and German businessmen. The Odessa City Charter, approved on 30 April 1863, was the most progressive in the empire, more democratic than those of St. Petersburg (1846) and Moscow (1862). No city in Russia had a greater ethnic diversity in its government.

For all its cosmopolitanism and freethinking, Odessa was primarily a Russian Orthodox city. Its special place as a major Orthodox center in southern Russia was determined by its role in pilgrimages to the Holy Land: the route to Palestine went through Odessa. Pilgrims from the "inner provinces" were provided with special inns and hospitality. In the nineteenth and early twentieth

Church of the Protection, destroyed 1930s. Postcard, 1900s.

centuries many churches were built, including the Church of the Protection (Pokrovsky) on Alexandrovsky Prospect (it has not survived), the Church of the Assumption, on Preobrazhenskaya Square (now the cathedral), and St. Ilya's on Pushkinskaya Street.

The Spaso-Preobrazhensky (Transfiguration) Cathedral and Cathedral Square were the center of the spiritual and social life of old Odessa, the site for the start of all significant events: church and state holidays, the procession of the cross at Easter, the reception of the city's important guests, including members of the Romanov dynasty and foreign crowned heads. Back in 1795, the foundations were laid for the Cathedral of St. Nicholas, which was under construction by the military engineer Vanrezant from the design of the architect Frapolli until 1808. Then the main altar was blessed in honor of the Transfiguration of the Lord, and that is why the church is named for the Transfiguration rather than St. Nicholas. In 1837 a belfry was built near the main building, which was later connected to the church. In that same year, the church became a cathedral, because Odessa became the see of the archbishop of Kherson and Taurida. The church was rebuilt many times up until 1900–1903. Highly revered national relics were preserved there: the miracle-working icon of the Kasperovskaya Mother of God, the ancient image of Odessa's heavenly protector, St. Nicholas Mirlikiisky, *Trinity* by the famous painter Paul Leroix, copies of the ancient "Korsyn" icons, a copper cross cast from coins donated by soldiers of the Crimean War, war trophy Turkish banners bestowed by the emperor, and so on. All

Spaso-Preobrazhensky Cathedral. Postcard, 1900–1910s.

Procession of the cross along a bridge. Postcard, early 1900s.

the bishops of the parish were buried in the cathedral, as well as Prince M. S. Vorontsov and his wife. In the mid-1930s the Spaso-Preobrazhensky Cathedral was destroyed by Soviet ideologues, along with an enormous number of other houses of worship and monasteries. However, at that time, the remains of the Kherson archbishops were reburied at the Svyato-Uspensky Monastery on Bolshoi Fontan and the Vorontsovs were moved to a remote cemetery in the suburb of Slobodok.

Many of Odessa's streets were once known for the specific type of buildings on them. For instance, The street floors along Alexandrovsky Prospect were all occupied by manufacturers and stores, Lanzheronovskaya was the street for ship companies, and Malaya Arnautskaya had five synagogues. Even one of the city's central avenues, Pushkinskaya, had two synagogues. In one, the synagogue of jewelers, young Vladimir Jabotinsky said memorial prayers for his father; he later became a well-known Zionist leader, journalist, and writer. Most Odessa synagogues were subdivided

by the profession of the majority of congregants: there were synagogues of clerks, coachmen, tailors, bakers, shoemakers, et cetera. In all, at the turn of the nineteenth century, Odessa had around seventy synagogues for a Jewish population of over 100,000, though most were in small rented or donated buildings.

The first synagogue of the city, where the Odessa Jewish community invited Rabbi Iztkhok Rabinovich from the nearby Moldavian town of Bendery, was built on the corner of what is now Rishelyevskaya and Evreiskaya Streets at the end of the eighteenth century. For over half a century on holidays and regular days, morning and evening, the Jews of Odessa prayed in that small, one-story building. It eventually became unusable and was torn down. In 1859 the new Main Synagogue, designed by the Italian Odessa architect F. Morandi, was built on the same spot—a magnificent two-story edifice in the Florentine style with Romanesque elements. Forty years later, the building was reconstructed and the date "1899" marked in the mosaic floor of the vestibule.

Above: Workshop of Jewish headstone masons, 1900s. *Right:* Undertaker.

Left: Odessa Jew at prayer, 1870s. Photograph by Jean Raoul.
Above: Sewing factory subsidized by local relief society, 1920s.

In 1841, settlers from Austria, particularly from the city of Brody, opened their own synagogue, called the Brodsky Synagogue. In 1863, the descendants of the original settlers built a new synagogue (design by F. Kolovich) on the corner of Italyanskaya and Pochtovaya (now Pushkinskaya and Zhukovskogo), a majestic building with an unstuccoed façade in the Gothic-Florentine style and with four stone cupola-covered pillars at the corners. The Brodsky Synagogue is inextricably associated with the rabbi who moved from Lvov, doctor of philosophy Shimon Shvabakher, a luminary in the history of Odessa's Jewish community. For many years, the synagogue's cantor was Nisan Blumental, known far beyond Odessa, and later followed by the famous Pinkhas Minkovsky, who was lovingly known as Pinya and whom Isaac Babel depicted in a short story. Minkovsky served at the synagogue for twenty years, but after the Russian Revolution left for America, realizing that no good would come from the new regime; he died in 1924 and was buried in Philadelphia. During Minkovsky's reign as cantor, David Novakovsky was conductor of the choir. His descendants live in the United States today. Minkovsky's enchanting voice, Novakovsky's musical compositions, the large choir, and the organ all created the fame of the Brodsky Synagogue, which was a spiritual center for the Jewish intelligentsia of Odessa.

In 1893 the merchant Moisei Kark funded a modest but graceful one-story synagogue for tailors on Remeslennaya (now Osipova) Street, and in 1909 on Zemskaya Street a wealthy

The Main Synagogue. Architect, F. Morandi, 1859.

mutual aid society of merchants and kosher butchers erected an impressive synagogue of unstuccoed local limestone, with decor of red brick, reminiscent of the medieval synagogues of Western Europe. Around the same time a huge synagogue architecturally atypical for Odessa appeared on Ekaterininskaya Street, near the famous Privoz Marketplace. It was destroyed in 1918 during Civil War artillery fire on the city. During the Soviet period, most of Odessa's synagogues were closed down and used for various nonreligious purposes. The return of synagogues, as well as churches, began only with the collapse of the Soviet Union. Jewish cemeteries in old Odessa were not only a final resting place but witnesses to many tragic events. The oldest of the known Jewish cemeteries appeared in the region of the future suburb near the Khadzhibeisky Liman in the eighteenth century, as evidenced by the epitaph of "pious mistress Dvosi, daughter of Rabbi Abram," buried in March 1770. The cemetery was preserved for more than 150 years and was barbarically destroyed during the occupation of the Rumanian army in World War II. The headstones were knocked down and the land plowed up.

On the territory of the city proper, the Old (First) Jewish Cemetery was founded beyond the porto-franco line in 1793. One of the first Odessa Jews buried there was Rabbi Meer, son of Itskhok Galevy. This cemetery accepted thousands of Odessa Jews: clergy, craftsmen, merchants, teachers, dockworkers, architects, office workers, journalists, store owners, and musicians who helped create Odessa's unique atmosphere and left behind modest

The Brodsky Synagogue. Architect, F. Kolovich, 1863. Lithograph, 1910.

Cantor Minkovsky and boys' choir in the Broadway Synagogue, early 1910s.

tombstones, pompous monuments of the wealthy, or severely designed family vaults. One epitaph reads: "Here lies David-Zalman Ashkenazi, banker son of a banker, grandson of a banker." At the same cemetery, in accordance with religious law, were buried the sacred scrolls of the Torah, defiled and torn up during a pogrom.

The Old Jewish Cemetery was spared until 1936, when the Soviets laid out a park there and on the neighboring Christian and Muslim cemeteries. All that is left of that first cemetery is a sad memory, a few photographs of ancient tombstones, and a mention in a novel by Osip Rabinovich.

In 1856, not far from the still extant first cemetery, on the road to Lustdorf, the German colony, the Second Jewish Cemetery was opened, surrounded by a stone wall with graceful pilasters. Beggars usually sat on the wall, waiting for funeral processions. Since this cemetery is more recent, we know many names of those

buried there: the founder of literature in Yiddish, Mendele Mocher Sforim; the writer Lazar Karmen, known as the "Odessa Gorky"; the talented poet Semyon Frug; the lawyer Isaac Khmelnitsky, with the same surname as the Ukrainian hetman; the founder of the Odessa first-aid station, Professor Yakov Bardakh; the architect Adolf Minkus, prototype for a character in Konstantin Paustovsky's novella; the accounting teacher Khaim Serebryany; the entrepreneur and representative of world-famous manufacturers of agricultural technology Emmanuil Babel, father of the writer Isaac Babel, who was executed during the years of Stalinist terror.

Hard times and the tragic events of the first quarter of the twentieth century left graves in the second cemetery of those who perished during the bloody Jewish pogrom of 1905, and those who died of starvation and typhus or were executed during the Civil War of 1918–20.

Destroyed memorial on the grave of Isaac Babel's father at the Second Jewish Cemetery, 1960s.

Grave fragments at the Second Jewish Cemetery, 1960s.

Headstone stella at the First (or Old) Jewish Cemetery,
first quarter of the nineteenth century.

Self-defense unit members of the Bund surrounding three slain comrades, October 1905.

But eventually, the Second Jewish Cemetery shared the bitter fate of the First. In 1978, it was bulldozed and replaced by a small park. Only the memorial designed by Odessa architect Fyodor Troupyansky on the grave of the victims of the pogrom and a few coffins were moved to other cemeteries.

The Jewish population of Odessa felt the full brunt of the anti-Semitism of the Russian and Soviet authorities in many other ways. Jewish children were limited by the infamous 5 percent quota in educational institutions; Jews were banned from numerous positions in city government; it was forbidden to wear specifically Jewish clothing, for married women to shave their heads as religious law requires, and to hold wedding processions with music and lit candles in the streets. Even though this was compensated somewhat by the religious tolerance of local administrators interested in the active participation of Jews in Odessa's burgeoning trade and industry, the growing socioeconomic contradictions of society, the strengthening of Russian capital, and the development and spread of reactionary tendencies in national policies made Odessa's Jews more and more aware of the instability and uncertainty of their situation. But the most vile and bloody manifestations of aggressive anti-Semitism were the pogroms, which marked the entire history of old Jewish Odessa. And while the first few pogroms may have begun as the result of individual provocations or misunderstandings or out of economic rivalry, later they became a reflection and consequence of official anti-Jewish policies; the noninterference of the police and army during the bloodiest events is ample evidence of that.

The first Jewish pogrom in Russia took place in Odessa in 1821. The roots of the incident went back to Constantinople (Istanbul), and its tragic denouement came near the Greek church on Ekaterininskaya Street. In Constantinople, Turks killed the Greek patriarch, whose body was brought to Odessa for burial. After the funeral someone in the church started a rumor that allegedly Jews had a hand in the patriarch's killing. The pogrom began, and local Greeks and sailors from Greek ships in port were joined by other local residents. Over sixty Jews were killed. In a bitter stroke of irony, the pogrom of 1871 began near the same Greek church, when Jews were accused of stealing the cross from the church fence, which was later found inside the church. The Jewish community in Odessa lived through seven pogroms in all, the most horrible of which was that of October 18–22, 1905. The mob, armed with knives and firearms, ransacked Jewish stores and kiosks, so numerous at the New Market, burst into houses in the Jewish neighborhood of Moldavanka, broke windows, smashed furniture, and slashed pillows and eiderdowns. They rampaged everywhere there were Jewish homes, offices, workshops, synagogues, and schools. The victims numbered 299, from eighteen-month-old Iser Zeltser to eighty-year-old Shimon Tsimelzon. Several thousand people hid in the large grounds of the Jewish

Sergei Utochkin, famous athlete, one of Russia's first aviators.
Photograph, late 1890s.

Hospital, which was surrounded by sturdy stone buildings. The wounded were brought there, too, by doctors (of various religions) from the first-aid station. Among them was Professor Bardakh, well known throughout Odessa as the founder of the station. There were heroes of this pogrom, brave fighters of the Jewish self-defense units, who risked their lives to save helpless people. The legendary Odessa aviator Sergei Utochkin was severely wounded protecting an elderly man from the mob, on Pushkin-skaya Street. The pogrom of 1905 led to a sharp increase in the emigration of Odessa Jews to the United States and Palestine.

The history of Odessa is full of paradoxes. One is that the Orthodox Jewish leaders and village authorities had long considered it the center, if not the hotbed, of unacceptable assimilation and loss of faith. At the same time, Odessa, like no other city, played an outstanding part in the formation and establishment of Zionism. In 1882 the Odessa physician Lev Pinsker, who defended Sevastopol in the Crimean War of 1854, wrote a brochure called "Self-Emancipation," in which he claimed that Jews could "rid themselves of being eternal wanderers" only by obtaining their own "refuge country." In 1890 Pinsker headed the Palestine Committee, founded in Odessa, which was the first legal Palestinophile organization in Russia, collecting money to aid Jewish settlers in Palestine, supporting cultural and educational groups there, establishing agricultural colonies, publishing Zionist books and magazines, and making the first contribution to purchase land for the Jewish University in Jerusalem. A board member of the Palestine Committee was the leading writer and philosopher Asher Ginzberg, known under the pseudonym Akhad-kha-Am. The committee's final action was organizing the resettlement in Palestine of 650 Jewish intellectuals at the height of the Civil War in Russia.

The Guela Society, founded in Odessa in 1904, bought up land in Palestine in order to pass it on to the newborn Jewish state. Meir Dizengof, an engineer and entrepreneur, headed Guela and then moved to Palestine. He became one of the founders of the Jewish quarter near Yaffa, which later turned into the city of Tel Aviv, and was elected its first mayor.

The history of Jewish Odessa is impossible to imagine without Vladimir Jabotinsky. He was born on Bazarnaya Street, which ended in the old Odessa marketplace, and he lived, studied, wrote, was published, had his plays produced in the local theater, took part in the creation of self-defense units to protect Jews from pogroms, and founded a Jewish publishing house. In Odessa Jabotinsky accepted the ideology of Zionism, which determined the course of the rest of his life, his work, and fate. For Jews all over the world, he is an outstanding figure of Jewish history, a tireless fighter of national renaissance and a Jewish state. Throughout his difficult life, Jabotinsky cherished a tender, lyric, and romantic love for his city, which "dictated" pages of his marvelous novella, *The Five.*

In some periods the commercial stratum formed up to 75 percent or more of the citizenry. This was many times more than in other cities of the Russian Empire, resulting in a lopsided social pyramid with an absolute preponderance of merchants and bourgeoisie over all other categories. This gave rise to a unique system of civil relations and a mentality that resembled no other.

Large-scale foreign trade operations would have been impossible without an infrastructure of commercial shipping offices, insurance societies, credit and banking institutions, a commercial court, granaries, land transport, port management, navigational security, quarantines, customs, and so on. Another important link in this chain was the stock exchange. The Russian word for exchange, *birzha*, is a flexible concept, since it comes from the French *bourse*, which mean purse. Metaphorically, the exchange was the "purse of public labor." It was founded in Odessa on 30 October 1796, even earlier than the one in New York. One could say that the stock exchange formed Odessa, set the foreign trade

mechanism in motion, and served in the earliest period of the city's existence as the universal institution of commercial life. The exchange served as court, bank, transport office, insurance society, place for concluding deals, and even the first form of mass media. The *Birzhevye listki* was in fact Odessa's first newspaper. The early exchange meetings were something of a cross between an oriental bazaar and a get-together of Wild West frontiersmen in the United States. The motley crowd of dealers and traders was constantly shaken by emotional explosions, heart-rending wails of duped simpletons, and noisy multilingual arguments that often degenerated in fisticuffs. That is why the police chief with a platoon of sturdy troops was constantly on patrol there. Later, the relations among the local dealer, notary publics, and brokers took on more civilized forms, and the Odessa stock exchange became one of the most solid in Russia as well as beyond its borders.

Governmental privileges granted to the young and promising city, many years of porto-franco, and the tolerance of local administrators—De Ribas, Richelieu, Langeron, and Vorontsov—toward Jews along with the traditional Jewish entrepreneurial spirit brought their broad integration into trade and industry. At first, Jews led only in the small goods trade and the sale of *glintwein* (a heated, mulled wine), a trend that came from Europe. But by the middle of the nineteenth century, not only were Jewish shopkeepers selling many more varieties of goods, but there were Jewish-owned banking offices and trading structures, and the chief *Hofmakler* (or broker) of the Odessa exchange was Simon Bernshtein. Another Simon, Gurovich, represented London and Liverpool insurance firms in Odessa. In the first decade of the twentieth century, when Odessa had already turned into a major trade and industrial center of southern Russia, Jews handled close to 90 percent of the grain export and owned almost half the manufacturing companies of the city.

Jews owned limestone quarries, sawmills, and factories that manufactured tin, beds, lacquers and paints, wire, mirrors, soap, and foodstuffs. The largest steam mill in the city belonged to Mr. Weinshtein, and later was transformed into a modern mill; Konelsky's cigarette paper factory was known throughout Russia; the pastries of the Krakhmalnikov Brothers, descendants of the baker who was one of the first settlers of Odessa, were of European quality; and to this day Odessites call hand-spring scales "kanters," no longer remembering that they used to be manufactured by the Kanter factory.

Around 70 percent of the commission stores and agencies belonged to Jews, who were representatives for such world-known companies as Benz, Vacuum Oil, Solingen, Moser, Pathé, Zeiss, and Underwood. Mendelevich's "Passage" was the equal of the mini-malls of Paris; it had numerous stores and the offices of *Odesskie novosti*, the newspaper that printed the young Vladimir Jabotinsky. It was considered prestigious to buy watches, gold, and diamonds at the stores of Barzhansky or Purits, whose forefathers had been modest jewelers at the dawn of Odessa. Iron from the Raushverger Brothers' stores covered city roofs. Thousands of Odessites strolled around in ready-to-wear clothing "from Landesman" and watches "from Kokhrikht." Jewish craftsmen opened hundreds of workshops in Odessa, and Jews owned wine cellars, delicatessens, newspaper kiosks, photography salons, inns, pharmacies, and over half the "establishments of imported industry." Odessa's famous *binduzhniki*, celebrated in the stories of Isaac Babel, hauled stone, furniture, and grain on their heavy *bindugi* carts. Many of the well-known Jewish merchants, who formed over 60 percent of that respected stratum, were awarded the title of "honored citizen of Odessa," but only one-third of the recipients of that honor were Jewish. Sober-minded Jewish merchants, who tried to be in tune with the times, often educated their children to join the ranks of the Jewish intelligentsia. Among the progeny of merchants and entrepreneurs were the architect M. Reingerts, the artist F. Gozeiason, the composer M. Raukhverger, the writer Isaac

Friedrich Gross, *The Odessa Stock Exchange*, 1855. Lithograph.

Babel, and the poet Vera Inber, cousin of the Bolshevik leader Leon Trotsky.

Banking in Odessa began with money changers seated at tables near the commercial casino in the house of Baron Reynaud, which served then as the stock exchange. The young city had a strong deficit of cash, sometimes unable to pay the salaries of the local garrison. In these conditions, the money changers helped the citizenry: they accepted the heterogeneous crowd's francs and pounds, liras and piastres, even the exotic *tangas* of Bukhara, and gave them Russian rubles and kopecks in exchange.

The Odessa financial market was open from the start to the whole world. The city's very first bank, for instance, was founded by the French trader Fournier and the Livorno banker Geome in 1802. In the 1800s, the French also created the first credit-insurance society, and the initiative was taken up by Greek merchants. The French established the first commercial court

Left: A poster for stationer Ivan Makh, who supplied literally all the grade school, high school, and university students of Odessa with notebooks. Above: "A Thousand Greetings." Postal money transfer, 1907. Opposite page: Advertisement for M. Popov and M. Zamaria's Tobacco Factory in Odessa. Advertisement for I. V. Frenkel. Russia's best manufacturer of cigarette paper and holders for papirosy, Russian cigarettes.

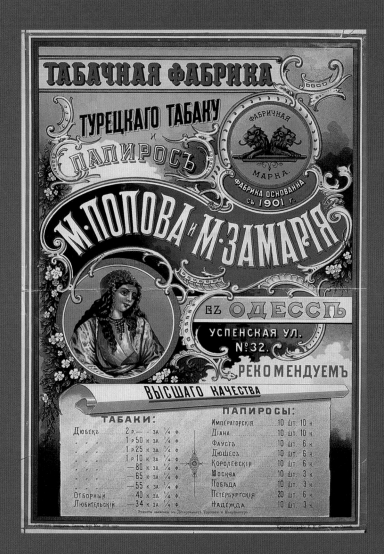

Advertisement for Iosif Konelsky's cigarette paper factory on Rishe-lyevskaya Street, 1904.

(1808) as well in Odessa. All the major Odessa bankers—Stiglietz, Rodokanaki, Rafalovich, and Mass—came from Europe. The office of the Russian State Bank was established in Odessa only in 1819–20 and did not start working until significantly later. The most important Odessa exporters for decades were almost all foreigners: besides those mentioned above, there were also Ralli, Kortazzi, Ponzio, Porreaux, Papudov, Viviani, Moberli, Trabotti, Inglesi, and Rubot.

In the second half of the nineteenth century, Odessa banking houses owned by members of the Jewish community had enormous authority in the Russian Empire and abroad: M. and E. Ashkenazi, A. Brodsky, M. Efrussi, A. Rafalovich, and O. Khais. The Odessa Ashkenazi were related to the greatest bankers in the world: Ginzburg, Warburg, Gerzfeld, von Girsch, and Eduard Rothschild himself. Rafalovich was the only magnate to go bankrupt, with a scheme to lower the credit ruble on the eve of the introduction of gold currency in Russia in 1890. Greek bankers—men like F. Mavrokordato and F. Petrokokino—always held serious positions on the financial market. Among the other major private credit institutions were the Land Bank of the Kherson Province, which gave long-term credit to landowners, the Bessarian-Tauride Bank, the Southern Russia Industrial Bank, the Odessa Discount Bank, and the Odessa branch of Crédit Lyonnais with a capital of 2.5 million francs.

The most important instrument for foreign trade operations in old Odessa was the porto-franco system, which lasted from 1819 to 1859. During this period, Odessa was the cheapest place to live in Russia. In fact, imported goods were taxed, but at a rate much lower than in other ports. The introduction of porto-franco spurred a huge influx of imported goods into Odessa. Trade turnover reached tens of millions of gold rubles. Odessa became the largest grain exporter in the world. The border of the porto-franco territory is fixed in the name of Straportofrankovskaya (Old Porto-Franco) Street and corresponds with the border of the historical

Advertisement for the Odessa showroom for Benz automobiles on Politseiskaya Street, 1899.

Advertisement for the Usher Landesman factory and store of ready-made clothing on Politseiskaya Street, 1899.

Above and opposite: Krakhmalnikov
Chocolate Wrappers, early 1900s.

center of the city. Two customs points were established on this border: the Kherson in Peresyp on the road leading to Kherson and Nikolayev and the Tiraspol in Moldavanka on the road to Tiraspol, Bendery, and Kishinev. Past those points, the full duty had to be paid on goods being brought out of Odessa. To hinder smuggling, the porto-franco border was fortified by a deep and wide ravine.

Count Mikhail Semyonovich Vorontsov (1782–1856) played a great role in the development of Odessa and all of New Russia. As the plenipotentiary for New Russia and Bessarabia as of May 7, 1823, Vorontsov presided over large-scale socioeconomic transformation in the enormous province, which turned out to be successful. After Richelieu, he continued civilizing the surrounding area, settling it, building infrastructure, utilizing the natural resources, expanding trade, and patronizing people of arts and sciences.

Vorontsov's life passed in military field bivouacs. He fought in dozens of campaigns: in the Caucasus, in Bessarabia, Moldavia, Walachia, Bulgaria, Poland, Prussia, Pomerania, and France. He faced Bonaparte at Smolensk, was wounded at Borodino, and vanquished the French at Krasnoe and many other battles. After Paris fell, Vorontsov commanded the Russian expeditionary corps in France. The count was awarded all the highest Russian orders, received two diamond-encrusted gold sabers "For Bravery" and "For Taking Varna," and military orders of almost all European countries. This born soldier was also a subtle diplomat, a man of enormous erudition who knew Latin and spoke all the basic European languages (he was brought up in London where his father was the Russian ambassador). He

Mignon chocolate from the Krakhmalnikov Brothers factory on Sredne-Fontanskaya Road, 1910s.

established learned societies, public libraries, and museums in Odessa and the region, organized the publication of newspapers, calendars, and book publishing in general, and opened many educational institutions.

Vorontsov was also a great humanitarian. He was constantly concerned about the welfare of people of other religions, primarily Jews and Tatars, working to improve their social and legal positions and promoting their education. Yet he is remembered by many unjustly for sending the exiled poet Alexander Pushkin back to his estate in Mikhailovksoe (Pskov Gubernia). The relationship between Vorontsov and Pushkin is usually reduced to a personal animosity based on jealousy over Vorontsov's wife, Elizaveta Ksaveryevna.

Although there are not many statues in Odessa, both Vorontsov and Pushkin are so honored. The passage of time put things in perspective, giving their due to Russia's greatest poet and her brave soldier and transformer. During his sojourn in Odessa, Pushkin worked on several epic poems and wrote numerous other poems. Surviving is a fragment of the manuscript for *Eugene Onegin*, with drawings he made in the margins of Odessa acquaintances—the Vorontsovs, Vasily Tumansky, Amalia Riznich, the corsair Morali, and other well-known people.

Pushkin had been exiled from the capital for what another poet in a different era called "a slap in the face of public taste." In the Soviet era much was made of his ties with the Decembrists, who called for a constitutional monarchy, turning him almost into a radical. Actually, when Pushkin graduated from the Tsarskoe Selo Lycée and found himself in the swirl of social life, the impulsive and emotional young poet did not control "either tongue or pen." He said and wrote what he felt in the face of treachery, hypocrisy, and despotism. Thanks to the intervention of friends, the poet was sent "to reform" not in Siberia, but in the still wild southwest region of the Russian Empire.

Ever since the days of Richelieu, Langeron, and Vorontsov, Odessa's populace never showed unanimity when it came to entertainment. It was not so much a social issue as a question of national and religious traditions, mores, manners, preferences, and prejudices. The only universal social salon was the City Theater.

Public masquerades and balls were rather infrequent. Unlike Moscow and St. Petersburg, Odessa preferred masquerades to balls. Masquerades in Odessa took place at the City Theater, the Club House of Baron Reynaud, later the Stock Exchange hall, and also in elite salons—the homes of such people as the Vorontsovs, Langerons, and Naryshkins. The variety of costumes amazed visitors: face cards, all kinds of historical figures, dwarves and giants, epic characters, ladies and gentlemen of the court of all periods and nations. The Odessa masquerades allowed for innovations and anachronisms. The solemn procession of masks (the prologue) could be accompanied by an intentionally ironic minuet instead of the traditional polonaise: the slower tempo was better for showing off the exquisite costumes. If there were a great many masks, the dance was repeated in a different tone and then once again in the original. Sometimes, it was just the ordinary polka. Then the masks moved around and met one another, in the waltz and mazurka. The waltz in those days was slower— not like the Viennese waltz. It was intended to warm people up for the mazurka and cotillion. Yet another southern innovation was to have the mazurka sometimes preceded by the quadrille, as a palliative to the cotillion, which usually served as the finale of every ball. The national coloration of the dances (polonaise and mazurka, Polish; waltz, German; quadrille and its variant, cotillion, French) pleased the crowd, giving everyone an opportu-

Mendelevich's "Passage" on Deribasovskaya, 1900s. Architect, L. Vlodek; designers, S. Milman and T. Fisher.

nity to shine. Some musical numbers, including the old-fashioned waltz, were done with vocals by soloists from the Italian opera. In the intermissions, there were buffets of simply champagne. The masquerades ended with the cotillion, a modernized quadrille in the tempo of a fast waltz. The cotillion embodied the carnival and represented the very spirit of young Odessa—cosmopolitan, temperamental, and filled with dignity and optimism. The dance steps were interrupted by games of forfeits or individual plays, which sometimes recapitulated the previous dance series: polonaise, waltz, mazurka. This was an imitation of the old-fashioned French carousel quadrille.

In the olden days the simple folk enjoyed the festival under the swings, funded by the city on holidays. May First was always marked by picnics on the cliffs. Each community—German, Italian, Greek, and so on—set up an area on the shore to cook traditional foods, drink, sing folk songs, and dance. The nobility gathered in the luxurious dachas outside town—belonging to the

№ 27 Одесса. Дума и Памятникъ Пушкину.
Odessa. La mairie et le monument Pouchkine.

Monument to Pushkin (unveiled on April 16, 1899).

Langerons, Sturdzes, Kortazi, Reynauds, Kobles—where professional orchestras and vocalists entertained. The Jewish and Karaite families celebrated holidays very privately. The Karaite women had a day a week at the bathhouse, where in the oriental tradition they pampered themselves, brushed one another's hair and plaited it in numerous small braids.

Unlike Moscow, St. Petersburg, and other northern cities, Odessa had Greek and Turkish coffeehouses, German bakeries, and Italian casinos, and people played *nardy* (dice) on the street. Lotto, which like dominos came from Italy, caught on early. It did not become fashionable in the north of Russia until the 1840s and was officially banned for a while as a form of gambling. Billiards was a game enjoyed by all strata of society, played by the major wholesalers as well as by the city's aristocrats—for instance, in Vorontsov's salon. The card playing center was the commercial casino at first and later moved to the English Club. The most popular card game was ombre (lomber), also an Italian national game. Of course, other card games were popular—whist as well as the gambling games of stoss, faro, and banco. But Odessa's favorite games were those requiring skill rather than luck. For a long time, playing cards smuggled in from Italy were preferred to Russian-made decks.

There were many card sharps in Odessa, and one of the most famous was the King of Spades, an Armenian. He cheated by marking the cards with phosphorus matches and wearing dark glasses. But once the candles went out in the room where he was playing, and his secret was revealed. The King of Spades barely got out of there. Another famous card player was the Polish Jew Abrashka. No one has learned how he cheated, though it is known that he soaked his jacket in some chemical that allowed him to distinguish red cards from black.

The ladies' world of old Odessa did not resemble that of other Russian cities. Women from St. Petersburg, Moscow, and other cities remarked on the extraordinary (to them) combination of

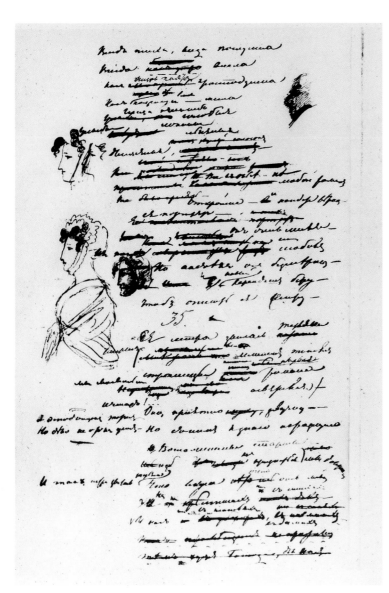

Facsimile of Puskin's manuscript pages, 1900s. Odessa Literature Museum.

noble aristocrats and merchant families in high society. While ladies from the merchant stratum did not feel very comfortable in society's salons at first, the women of Odessa freed themselves of social prejudices much sooner than their contemporaries in Russia's two main cities. Moreover, the wealthiest wholesalers' wives quickly overtook their noble rivals, and their homes became the centers of the local beau monde.

One of the brightest examples of the burgeoning bourgeoisie was the great Odessa beauty, the Greek Ariadna Evstratyevna Papudova, née Sevastopoulo. Her marriage to Konstantin Fotyevich Papudov was a profitable alliance of two major business families. Papudov exported grain and his charming spouse reigned at balls, masquerades, and social events. All the great social lions fell in love with her—not only in Odessa, but in Paris: from the richest Odessites, Marazli, to Baron Rothschild, who gave Ariadna the Palais de Sagan on the Champs Élysées. When she gave balls at her enormous house on Sobornaya Square, she invited 500–600 guests. Ariadna died over a century ago, yet Odessites to this day refer to the house as Papudova's House.

The most popular shopping places were department stores, known as English stores. They sold wares from Germany and France as well, and later from the United States. Amazingly, many of these items still serve the grandchildren and great-grandchildren of the original buyers. Today, in the old family homes one can find coffee grinders, dishes, cigar cases and snuff boxes, statuettes, clocks, and furniture bought at Bellino-Fenderikh, the Stieffel brothers, William Wagner, or Petrokokino many decades ago. And to this day, hat boxes from Mlle Ozerskaya, of ladies' traveling boxes from Mme Straz, and delicate laces from Mrs. Grange, or Lecour and Mangen, live out their long lives. In the homes of senior citizens one can still find bottles and jars from the cosmetic firm of Gudshon and Kokhler.

Jewish, Greek, and French charitable organizations were consistently the largest philanthropic entities in the city. As early

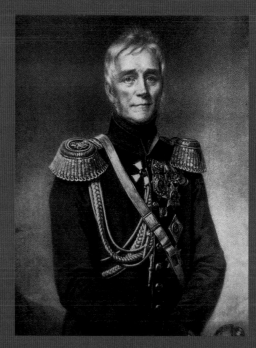

Clockwise: Odessa's legendary Grigory Marazli. Photo, 1870s; Serene Count M. S. Vorontsov in the later years of his life; Countess Elizaveta Vorontsova; Countess Roksandra Edling, founder of a large-scale charitable movement in Odessa. Engraving, 1844; Portrait of A. E. Papudova by Rudolf Feodorovets, 1860s.

ОДЕССА.—ODESSA. № 105.
Еврейская общественная больница.—L'hôpital public israélite.

г. ОДЕССЫ.

СТОЛОВАЯ ДЕШЕВОЙ КУХНИ № 1.

Above: Jewish Hospital on Gospitalnaya Street. Postcard, early 1900s.
Right: Meal at Subsidized Kitchen
no. 1, Society for Aid to the Needy,
15 October 1929.

as October 1798 the Jewish community had created a fund for widows and orphans, and in 1802 it opened a Jewish hospital. In Odessa's first few years the city opened an orphanage. Later, an enormous role was played by the Women's Benevolent Society, created on the initiative of Countess Roksandra Skarlatovna Edling (née Sturdzy) and Countess Elizaveta Ksaveryevna Vorontsova (née Branitskaya). This philanthropic institution, which supported needy citizens in the lean years of poor harvest, cemented civil society by bringing together members of the nobility and merchant class. Good deeds united Odessites who were separated by existing rules and prejudices. In the early 1890s, the city had almost a hundred institutions, shelters, buildings with cheap apartments, soup kitchens, mutual aid societies, and so on. Besides the powerful Jewish and Greek philanthropic organizations, Odessa had very effective Austro-Hungarian, Italian, German, Serbian, French, Bulgarian, and Swiss philanthropic societies and aid offered by various houses of worship.

Not counting the Vorontsovs, who gave almost three million rubles to charity, Grigory Grigoryevich Marazli (1831–1907) was the greatest philanthropist in Odessa, donating money, land, and buildings to the city. He financed the construction of hospitals, orphanages, public schools, libraries, and churches, and he gave the city a palace which was turned into the Museum of the Society of Fine Arts. Between 1878 and 1895 Marazli served as the mayor, during which period the ground was broken for Alexandrovsky Park, the *konka* (horse-drawn trains) and the steam trolley were initiated, a new City Theater was built, and many educational and medical institutions appeared. Marazli also donated a lot of money to his historical homeland, Greece, and at his own expense had the Russian classics translated and published in Greek.

For all his good works, Marazli was an epicurean, and there are many tales of his amorous adventures. The women in his life included Eugénie Marie de Montijo, wife of Napoleon III. He was very close to Sarah Bernhardt, and courted all the great beauties

Musical evening at the dacha of Countess Langeron. Lithograph by Friedrich Gross, mid-nineteenth century.

of Odessa—Papudova, Brodskaya, and Zarifi. He did not marry until 1903, when he "stole" the wife of the chairman of Odessa's Commercial Court. According to Greek historian Augitides, Marazli died of syphilis.

Jewish philanthropy was quite diverse. Abram Brodsky, head of a major trading company, donated a two-story stone building in the middle of town for a new orphanage, the banker Efrussi financed the construction of the City School, the merchant Kogan maintained a building where the poor could live for almost nothing, and Jewish doctors, who made up over a third of the city's physicians, treated the poor for free. Every more or less well-to-do and well-known Jew in the city considered it a duty to give as much as he could and an honor to be a member of the board of some charitable institution, of which there were a great many.

The oldest charitable institution was the Jewish Hospital, opened in 1802 on a street later named Gospitalnaya. The hospital's expenses were covered by the "box collection" (tax on kosher meats sold in the city) and donations of benefactors, who paid for entire hospital wings. The hospital often treated patients for free, no matter what their religion.

In the early twentieth century the city had several dozen charitable institutions and mutual aid societies: a home for poor Jewish unwed mothers, orphanages, homes, soup kitchens, funeral funds, commissions to hand out free matzo, and professional associations that aided tailors, clerks, members of synagogue choirs, watchmakers, students at various schools, et cetera. There was usually a surge of philanthropy after tragic events in the lives of Odessa's Jews. Jewish philanthropy in Odessa was a complete system of social aid, with people from all walks of life able to find help.

The history of Jewish public education in Odessa is only a bit younger than the city, since from the start the new settlers included a large number of teachers from *cheders*, traditional Jewish schools. By the end of the eighteenth century besides the cheders, there was a Talmud-Torah and in 1866 the "higher school of Judaism" appeared, the Odessa yeshiva, where the great poet Haim Byalik taught Hebrew. But as early as 1926 the Jews of Odessa realized that in a European city Jewish education could not be limited to cheders and opened a Jewish public school. It was the first school in Russia that offered, besides traditional Jewish disciplines, Russian, German, and French, mathematics, biology, geography, history, and accounting. The leading source of technical education for the Jewish community was the Trud Society's school, which opened in 1864 thanks to the active support of Rabbi Shvabakher. Located in its own building, it had auditoriums and workshops (carpentry, mechanical, metalwork). There were also evening classes for adults in drafting, arithmetic, geometry, physics, and the basics of technology. And people could graduate as fully qualified masters.

By 1917 Odessa had become one of the largest centers in Russia of Jewish education. Through the efforts of scholars, educators, religious and civic figures, writers, and philanthropists, a network of public education was created, including cheders, three Talmud-Torahs (one of which was headed by the writer Mendele Mocher Sforim), a yeshiva, a high school, general education schools, professional schools, trade, midwifery, and dentistry institutions, and various courses in music, arts, accounting, calligraphy, stenography, cutting, and sewing.

Jewish youth were taught in non-Jewish institutions as well: Lev Pinsker studied at the famous Richelieu Lycée, the artist Leonid Pasternak at the art school, the poet Benedikt Livshitz at New Russia University, Isaac Babel at the commercial school, the poet Eduard Bagritsky at agricultural courses, and Vladimir Jabotinsky at the Richelieu Gymnasium. This was the most prestigious of the state high schools, and in the 1910s another famous Russian writer, though of Polish origins, studied there, Yuri Olesha. The general cultural level of Odessa's Jewish community was raised to a great degree by the Jewish libraries, including the library of the Society of Jewish Clerks with its large book collection. The excellent Jewish public education had an influence on the formation of the national intelligentsia: more than 30 percent of the local doctors, 30 percent of engineers, and 70 percent of lawyers were Jewish.

On the whole, the high level of culture, literature, and education in Odessa combined with the city's European orientation was one of the reasons that many people who lived in Odessa achieved world fame: poet Anna Akhmatova; poet and artist David Burlyuk; artist Wassily Kandinsky; and pianist Sviatoslav Richter.

Mail service was established in Odessa in early May 1794, even before the official founding of the city. In the first few decades, the mail stations were in private houses, in space rented by the post office. They had to be in a stone building and have rooms for the supervisor, the coachmen, and separately for the passengers, as well as a large courtyard with stables and sheds and, especially, a

Clockwise from top left: Traditional Jewish school *(cheder),* 1900s; A group of
Jewish writers; Courses in skilled work at Sixth Professional School, "Metal,"
1930; A Jewish school, 1900s.

well. The mail was transported along two main mail roads to Kherson and Tiraspol by special coaches that traveled from station to station some 25 versts (km) apart. The tired horses were replaced with fresh ones, and the "marathon" continued. Private persons could use the mail troikas, but priority was given to government officials. The first postmark "Odessa" appeared under Richelieu, while round postmarks with a changeable date appeared only in the early 1830s. In those days four kinds of mail were sent from the city: extra-mail (three times a week), St. Petersburg ordinary, Dubossarksy, and Voznesensky (twice a week). The postage was 20 silver kopecks to Kherson Province, 30 kopecks to Bessarabia, 70 kopecks to Moscow Province, 90 to St. Petersburg, 100 kopecks, that is, 1 ruble, to Siberia. Until 1823 the post office rented private buildings, and then moved to its own building on the corner of Ekaterininskaya and Pochtovaya (today, Zhukovsky Street). In 1898 the Post Office building on Sadovaya Street was built. After sea communications were opened in 1828 with the Crimea, the Caucasus, and Turkey, mail was sent by ship, and in 1865 the coaches pulled by troikas were replaced by the railroad connecting Odessa with Balta and then on to the two capitals. In 1837, postage became the same wherever mail was going and in 1852 newspapers and magazines were delivered to Odessa by mail. The first mailboxes appeared on Odessa streets in April 1869, after one-rate stamps were introduced. Intercity mail was also delivered then. By 1875, there were twenty-five mailboxes. By the end of the nineteenth century there were five post offices in Odessa.

Where there is mail, there are stationery, paper, envelopes, and postcards. There were no fewer than twenty stationery stores in old Odessa. The best were located on Deribasovskaya Street (Ya. Barsky, G. Gezelle, and I. Pokorny), Preobrazhenskaya Street (I. Makh and F. Makh), Ekaterininskaya Street (N. Galperin), and Rishelyevskaya Street (I. Levinson). Traditionally many Jews and Germans owned stationery stores. Most of those listed specialized

The Richelieu Gymnasium. Early twentieth century.

in art supplies, photo albums, and postcards. As for Ivan Makh, he supplied all the grade school, high school, and university students of Odessa with notebooks.

For decades, placid and patient oxen faithfully served the grain trade, dragging heavy carts, filled to the brim with selected grains, for hundreds of kilometers through the dry, arid steppes. Only their incredible strength and endurance allowed the oxen to manage in the crowded and narrow streets of Odessa in the first half of the nineteenth century.

Odessa's wealth came at a high price. The citizens had to overcome not only epidemics and difficulties with supplies of water, fuel, and construction materials, but weather catastrophes, as well. Dust storms were followed by freezing ice storms, then flooding in the limans, which flooded the suburb of Peresyp.

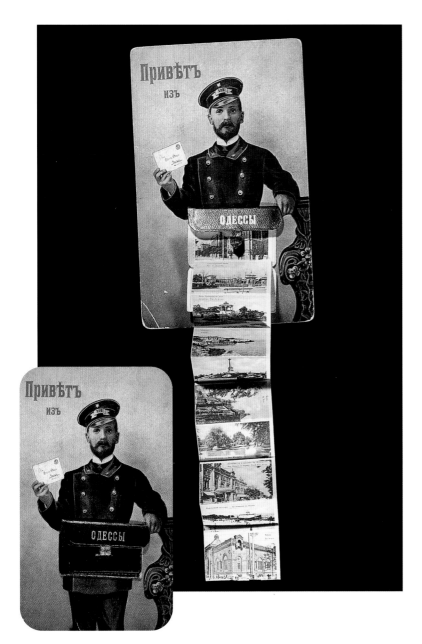

The omnibus, or tram-coach, was the first form of public transport in Odessa. Regular service was established in the summer of 1844 by Crocetti, an Italian company. The omnibuses traveled as a rule to the beach dacha locales—to the dacha of Countess Langeron, to the Botanical Gardens, to Maly Fontan, to Lustdorf, the German colony, on Kuyalnitsky Liman. The cost of a ride depended on the distance and varied from 10 to 80 kopecks in silver. Intercity travel in the mid-nineteenth century was done in diligences, a type of coach.

In the late nineteenth and early twentieth centuries, small steam engines, called *parovichki*, traveled to outlying dacha locations around Odessa. Later, the tracks were used for electric trolleys, and even today the roads leading to Bolshoi Fontan and Chernomorka (Lustdorf) are marked by sixteen stations. They refer not only to the names of trolley stops but to specific regions of the city's territory.

An old postcard captures a curious fact of the parallel existence in Odessa of both an electric trolley and the so-called *konka*, a passenger train drawn by horses along the tracks. The *konka* began in 1860, and the trolley in 1906–10. Both were in the hands of the Anonymous Belgian Stock Company. Because of the narrow streets, in some places the track was only one meter wide. Open (summer) cars had perpendicular wooden seats and the closed ones had seats along the walls. Before the revolution the total tracks added up to 75 versts (km). A paid ticket allowed a passenger to switch to different lines to a final destination.

In Pushkin's day, a steep path led down to the sea along the cliff from what is now Primorsky Boulevard. Later it was replaced by a light wooden staircase, then by the so-called Gigantskaya

Odessa mailman, early 1900s. Souvenir postcards.

The main hall of the city post office, built in 1896–98 on Sadovaya
Street. Architect B. F. Kharlamov.

(Gigantic) Stairs, now called the Potemkin Steps, and in 1902
a funicular was built parallel to it, designed by N. I. Pyatnitsky,
a young engineer and son of a high school director. At the same
time they planned the path of the future funicular; laid a one-
track rail about 100 meters long, with a branch in the middle;
built an airy wooden pavilion on the boulevard, and at the bottom
a stone building with a ticket office, platform, and office, and a
small power plant next to it; put together two 35-passenger cars
brought from Paris; and put in arcing lampposts along the road.
The funicular worked without any problems for over sixty years,
after which it was demolished for no good reason.

In 1891 the first car in Russia appeared on the streets of
Odessa—an early Benz belonging to V. V. Navrotsky, the editor and
publisher of the newspaper *Odesskii listok*. By the mid-teens, the
Benz company had opened a showroom on Rishelyevskaya Street
and almost twenty-five automobile companies were represented on
the market, including Mercedes, Studebaker, Ford, and Opel. Soon
there appeared car repair shops, automobile parts stores, second-
hand sales of cars, advertising by the Vacuum Oil Company of its
lubricants, and every self-respecting driver felt obliged to purchase
a leather jacket, cap, and gloves with fancy cutouts. The car was
becoming part of the lifestyle of Odessites, promoted in great part
by the Odessa Automobile Society, which opened in 1912 the First
Automobile Salon, an auto show in the European manner. Some
new fashionable buildings had red-brick garages, not without
architectural interest, in their courtyards. Carless lovers of the road
could rent automobiles, others could avail themselves of the services
of the Society of the Odessa Taximotor. Driving schools were
opened, and the first Lorelei car manufactured was given away as a
prize in a charity lottery. The newspapers, in a sad sign of the
times, ran items about road accidents.

Unlike other cities, where visiting barnstormers gave exhibition
flights on still-exotic airplanes, in Odessa Russian aviation took
wing, so to speak. As early as 1908 the Odessa air club was
founded, publishing magazines devoted to flying; they held Aviation Week and the First Southern Russian Congress of Air Flying
Business; and at the 1910 Trade and Industry Fair there was an
enormous air pavilion with a school for pilots—to this day citizens
of Odessa call it the "school aerodrome."

On 8 March 1910, Mikhail Efimov in a Farman airplane
soared into the sky from the hippodrome of the New Russia Society for the promotion of horse breeding. This was the first flight
in Russia of a Russian pilot and his name has been immortalized
in a poem by Alexander Blok. That same day Efimov also made
the first flight in Russia with a passenger, A. Anatra, president of
the air club. Soon after that, the great bicycle racer Sergei Utochkin, subsequently called the "Chalyapin of the air," took his "test
flight for the title of aviator pilot."

Top: Konka (horse-railroad) stop at the intersection of Richelyevskaya and Zhukovskogo. *Bottom:* Oxen were a unique form of city transport. Photo, late nineteenth century.

The stationery store and printing and lithography house of Ya. N. Barsky on Deribasovskaya Street, opposite the City (Deribasovsky) Gardens. A rare advertising postcard, 1900s.

Одесса. — Подземная машина.   Odessa. — Le faniculaire.

10 Одесса Станція Подъемной машины на Николаевскомъ Бульварѣ
Odessa Station de la funicilaire sur le Boulevard de Nicolas

Одесса. Поѣздъ прибывающій съ Фонтана.

No. 48. Одесса - Станція трамвая съ угла Нѣжинской и Тираспольской улицъ.
Odessa - Station du tramway vue du coin des rues Tyraspolskaya et Niechynskaya

Clockwise from top left: Omnibus/funicular. Funicular station, Boulevard St.
Nicholas; Trolley station at Tyraspolskaya and Niechynskaya; Steam train
arriving from Bolshoi Fontan. Postcards, early twentieth century.

Advertisement for Case (an American manufacturer) cars.

A legend in his lifetime, Sergei Isaevich Utochkin was an extraordinary man with many talents and interests, knowledgeable in technology and literature. His greatest passion was for sport in eccentric ways: he rode his bicycle down the Potemkin Steps, he flew a plane over the Pyramid of Cheops, he ran ten kilometers neck and neck with a steam trolley from the railroad station in Odessa to the Sixteenth Station at Bolshoi Fontan, and on skates he went through incredible figures, leaving on the ice his signature—Sergei Utochkin.

That same year marked the first flight by a Russian writer Alexander Kuprin, who went up with his friend, the aviator Ivan Zaikin. No longer in existence, the Anatra Airplane Factory, which employed over two thousand people, including the budding writer Ilya Il'f, produced about fifty planes a month by 1916. The popularity of aviation in Odessa was so great that the famous pastry plant of the Krakhmalnikov Brothers even produced a chocolate bar called Flying, with various types of airplanes on the wrapper. Today, some chewing gum manufacturers include inserts with colorful pictures of various cars, but the idea was born in Odessa.

Yet another male pastime in old Odessa was sailing. In the last quarter of the nineteenth century, two yacht clubs were established—the elite Chernomorsky and the more democratic Ekaterininsky. Periodically they held regattas in the direction of Ochakovo and beyond. There were also sculling races in Odessa Bay, with sterling silver cups for the winners.

Roller skates were known in Odessa for a very long time. According to memoirists, in the last decades of the nineteenth century trendsetters shocked society by appearing in public places, even balls, "on wheels." In the early twentieth century, the craze swept the entire city and local craftsmen began making skates in various designs. In 1909, according to the illustrated magazine *Sport i nauka (Sport and Science)*, "a rink has been opened in Odessa for 'roller-skating' [in English] (skates with wheels), well-equipped and with an experienced manager." Odessites called

Адр.-справочн. книга г. Одессы „РУССК. БЕДЕКЕРЪ". 3.

АВТОМОБИЛИ

КЕЙСЪ

ИЗВѢСТНЫ ПОВСЮДУ

КОМПАНІЯ МОЛОТИЛОКЪ
Ж. И. КЕЙСЪ
10 ул. ЖУКОВСКАГО   П. Я. 12-36.
Телефонъ № 11-04.

Case automobile advertising.

that artificial rink the Roll Palace. It was situated in the center of the city on Khersonskaya Street in the courtyard of the Grand Hotel, and soon became a favorite recreation spot. Unfortunately, the Revolution and Civil War destroyed the establishment forever.

Another characteristic of Odessa life was the popularity of public baths. The Italians turned the City Theater into a social salon, but the Eastern peoples preferred to socialize in smoky coffee houses and sumptuous steam baths designed like ancient Turkish models. The best bathhouses belonged to Karaites, who had moved to Odessa from Tatar and Turkish Crimea. The most famous bathhouse of Odessa was built by the Crimean Karaite Isaac Solomonovich Isakovich. In essence, this was a hydro spa, where citizens could take mineral baths with chemical content exactly like the waters of the major European spas—Carlsbad, Marienbad, Wiesbaden, and others. The Odessa baths in the oriental style had separate rooms for rest and socializing. There were Turkish divans along the walls, and tables bearing Eastern delicacies were rolled up to them. The customers could also have coffee and a hookah. Business and politics were discussed in the baths and deals were made in the private rooms. The cost varied from 25 to 75 kopecks.

At the intersection of Deribasovskaya and Ekaterininskaya streets, in the fashionable center of town, stood the most popular hairdressing salon of old Odessa. It belonged to brilliant French coiffeurs—first Trinité and then Lavignotte. In imitation of Parisians, local barbers took on French names—Jean, Basil, Felix—which they used in their foreign-language signs. However, the city authorities waged a campaign against this mystification and forced them to reveal their true names, such as Kirkor, Agafon, Pantelei, and Ivan.

The popularity in old Odessa of beer halls and excellent breweries was due to the German community. The most popular beer halls were Rotte and Nikolai, both on Deribasovskaya Street, Stepanov's on Rishelyevskaya, and later the famous Gambrinus. Odes-

Advertisement for the Anatra Airplane Factory, 1910s.

Roller skaters in 1900s. Postcard.

The baths belonging to Isaac Isakovich on Preobrazhenskaya, late nineteenth century.

sites readily consumed the beer of local breweries—Santsenbakher (later TOPZ, from the initials of the Society of the Odessa Brewery), Kempe, and Enni. National brands, like Moscow's Trekhgornoe and St. Petersburg's Kalinkin, were also good sellers.

In 1894 colorful posters appeared in Odessa advertising a circus named after Santsenbakher, the local beer king. Naturally, the owner of the largest brewery in the city did not appear in the ring with a lion tamer's whip or in a clown's orange wig. He paid for the construction of a circus (engineer A. Gelfand) on his land next to the New Market. People called it Santsenbakher's iron circus, because the big top was constructed of metal. Santsenbakher's circus was not the first in Odessa, but his predecessors were situated in random locations not expressly built for a circus. Although Odessa was never known as a major circus city, the famous Russian clown Durov, his Italian colleague Giacomino, and the Truzzi animal tamers all performed at the new circus. The arena was also used for championship bouts of French wrestling, which was wildly popular and which was more like theater than sport. The writer Kuprin always attended the Odessa circus on his frequent visits to the city; he found many subjects for his stories there. The circus's huge hall was used for other entertainments, including rallies and showings of what were then called cinematographic pictures.

Odessites liked calling their city "Little Paris." One of the similarities with the French capital was the presence of cafés, colorful and festive, with graceful verandas or tables simply placed under plantains and acacias on shady, picturesque streets. Every period had its well-known café, which, even after they ceased to exist, remained in the city's history: the Greek coffee shops of Pushkin and Gogol's day; the Italian café and pastry shop of Zambrini, where Chekhov came for the famous ice cream; Robin's café, with its special room for chess; and the Swiss Fanconi Café, which was a landmark of old Odessa. It existed from 1872 until the beginning of the Revolution of 1917, when the last owner emi-

The hairdressing salon of Trinite-Lavignotte, at the intersection of
Ekaterininskaya and Deribasovskaya streets, 1870s.

Advertisements for the F. Enni and Company brewery in Odessa.

grated. At first, the café was a hangout for card sharps and shady businessmen, but gradually it became a kind of club for local and visiting writers, artists, actors, and athletes. One could see sitting on the veranda, which faced the noisy and colorful Ekaterininskaya Street near Primorsky Boulevard, A. I. Kuprin, I. A. Bunin, the young Isaac Babel, Vladimir Mayakovsky, and David Burlyuk, in town to give readings. The café is mentioned in folk songs and there isn't a writer who described Odessa at the turn of the century who did not mention the Fanconi. Even the culture of smoking differed in Odessa from the rest of Russia. Pushkin had sung the praises of the local Greek and Turkish coffee houses, where the customers smoked hookahs and pipes. There was nothing similar in St. Petersburg or Moscow, naturally. Besides which, Odessa—unlike the two capitals of Russia—permitted smoking in the streets and in public places. Visitors thought this very democratic. The best brands of aromatic Turkish tobacco were sold very reasonably in the period of porto-franco—20–40 kopecks a pound. In the second half of the nineteenth century, Odessa became a major tobacco-processing center, manufacturing pipe tobacco, various brands of cigarettes, and tobacco paper.

The famous Privoz Market—noisy, slightly crooked, and ethnically diverse—was yet another visiting card of both old and new Odessa. Here today, as a hundred years ago, untranslatable Odessa jokes arise and several generations of satirists have found inspiration. The other main prerevolutionary bazaars—the Old and New—were stationary and with foundations: they had stone pavilions, stalls, stores, and warehouses. For many decades the Privoz was only a square where farmers sold their goods from carts and wagons. The Russian word *privozit'* means "to bring by transport," and local agricultural regions brought their wares to the Privoz. Gradually the market became so popular that people started to construct stone and wooden buildings. Eventually an architectural glory, the Fruit Passage, was built. The sales statistics at Privoz show that in the late nineteenth century Odessa annually consumed 1,132,800 chickens and 40 million eggs.

Many cities experience a summer lull: office workers go on vacation, the theater season ends, and schools and universities are closed. But Odessa came alive in the summer. Resorts, dachas, and rooming houses were filled with thousands of locals and visitors thirsting for sea bathing, hot sun, and the medicinal mud baths of Kuyalnitsky Liman. Ever since Pushkin's day in the early 1800s, aristocrats from St. Petersburg, Moscow, and other large cities came to Odessa to rest and take the cure, including such people as Zinaida Volkonskaya, Vera Vyazemskaya, and Olimpiada Shishkina. Many families, such as

Advertisement for the Society of the Odessa Brewery (TOPZ), formerly the Santsenbakher Brewery, 1910s.

the Meyendorfs, Stenbok-Fermors, and Demidov-San-Donatos, built seaside houses.

New bathing spots, shooting ranges, and bowling greens appeared at the famous Langeron Beach, located on the site of the former governor-general's dacha, and in Arcadia, the fashionable park, and on the picturesque Golden Shore in the suburb of Bol-shoi Fontan. The sound of music floated over Primorsky Boule-vard on quiet summer evenings, for a band played near the statue of Richelieu, fireworks blazed in the black sky, and the stages of summer theaters glowed invitingly. There was a wooden theater on Kuyalnitsky Liman that held fifteen hundred, and the famous architect Yu. Dmitrenko built a summer theater near Langeron Beach. As early as 1892 the first such theater appeared on Bolshoi Fontan, where the actors played on a small, dimly illuminated stage and the undemanding summer audience sat under a ply-wood roof that let in the whistle of a nearby steam engine, music

Advertisement for A. Michri Tobacco Factory in Odessa.

The veranda of the Café Fanconi on Ekaterininskaya Street. Architect, Yu. Dmitrenko, 1913. Postcard, 1910s.

Above: Privoz market, 1930s. *Opposite:* Advertisement for L. Abramov's Tobacco Factory in Odessa.

№					
№ 1	ქართული მარში	1		ვაჟკაცი	
„ 2	ვაჟკაცი	2		ენგურითგამი	
„ 3	მენახშირი	3		მეტივეითმი	
„ 4	სოლიო	4		ცინ რემართოუ	
„ 5	სირტაკი	5		ომი ხომ ოჩომ	
„ 6	თითი ძუძ	6		სამტრელოა	
„ 7	ხოგანი	7		ხოგანი	
„ 8	ლეკური	8		ლეკური	
	№ 1			№ 2	

НЕЧАДА Балковская № 191 ОДЕССА

Above and opposite: A vintage *sharmanka* (or portable organ)
used by wandering musicians.

Arcadia. Postcard, early 1910s.

from a neighboring restaurant, and dust, it seemed, from the entire region. In 1906 on the same site the architect B. Bauer built a capital theater with open galleries on both sides of the façade, an observation deck on the roof, its own power plant, a hall for 700 people, and a stage with the most modern equipment. Celebrated actors performed there and young, as-yet-unknown poets read their works.

Jews who moved to Odessa from cities and small towns of Central Europe and Ukraine brought not only their customs, mores, and styles, but also their music. Jewish folk musicians—klezmers—played at weddings, dances, and fairs. They assimilated melodies of other nations, mastered new musical instruments, and sometimes became professional performers. Peisakh (Peter) Stolyarsky, son of a village klezmer and a klezmer himself, graduated from the Odessa Music School and founded a children's music school with a unique method of developing talent in gifted children. He was the first teacher of the great twentieth-century violinist from Odessa, David

Oistrakh. Another pupil of Stolyarsky's school, in the class of Professor Berta Reingbald, was the world-famous pianist Emil Gilels.

Village klezmers taught Sedner Pevzner, the violinist who moved to Odessa and played in the Gambrinus beer hall in a cellar on Preobrazhenskaya Street. Unquestionably talented, he picked up melodies by ear instantly and pleased the customers by playing Jewish, Russian, Ukrainian, Georgian, English, and other tunes. His popularity was so great that his audience included stevedores from the port, poor Jewish craftsmen from Moldavanka, workers from the suburb of Peresyp, and foreign sailors—as Lazar Karmen, the aficionado of Odessa's lowlife, described it. The customers called him Sashka the Violinist. He was the subject of the talented writer and playwright Semyon Yushkevich, who wrote about the life of Odessa Jews and later died as an émigré in Paris. Another famous writer, Alexander Kuprin, met Sashka and wrote a marvelous short story about him, "Gambrinus," which was translated into many languages.

Klezmer melodies were the basis of many Odessa folk songs, like "Music Plays on Moldavanka" or "A Beer Hall Opened on Deribasovskaya." In klezmer ensembles of several people, there were usually no two musicians playing the same instrument, and so each musician played a kind of solo, improvising freely and carrying the melody. This manner of playing was like that of small Negro bands in New Orleans, the birthplace of American jazz. That is why the famous singer Leonid Utesov, and Odessite who loved his city, used to say that to some degree Odessa could be considered the birthplace of jazz and its progenitors the small Jewish klezmer "capellas."

Leonid Utesov, whose real name was Leib Vaisbein, started his stage career in Odessa by performing satirical and humorous ditties, Odessa songs stylized to sound like folk songs, in small theaters, particularly the Bolshoi Rishelyevsky. The authors of these songs were local vendors of "rhymed humor" such as, Miron Yampolsky, whose "The Wedding of Shneyerson"—about life

Daily Life in Odessa ~ III ~

in wartorn Odessa during the Civil War—was his greatest hit. Born in 1920, the song lived through the ages and was carried by émigrés to various countries. Today, in a small restaurant in Brooklyn or San Francisco you can often hear the galloping klezmer melody of "It's terribly noisy in the Shneyerson house."

There's truth in the joke that jazz was born in Odessa. In any case, the culture of street music is deeply rooted there. By the middle of the twentieth century, every self-respecting tavern had its own band (violin, clarinet, flute, horn, bass fiddle, and drum) or a "musical machine," that is, a mechanical organ. These organs were made in the city, at piano factories, which were owned primarily by people of German descent—Haas, Stapelberg, Raush, Opperman, Vitsman, Gershgeimer, Hek, and others.

Odessa pianos and "musical machines" were distributed throughout Russia. One popular instrument was the *sharmanka*. The name comes from the first line of a very popular song, "Charmante Katherine." The Ukrainian name for the instrument,

The framing mat from a fashionable photography studio.

Katerinka, comes from the song, too. The sharmanka was a portable organ without keyboard, used by wandering musicians (pp. 108–109). The Odessa factory gradually learned to put several dozen popular melodies into the music box: folk songs, waltzes, and opera hits. The organ grinders usually set up near bars or "houses of ill repute" and were subjected to moralizing lectures for exploiting pretty girls of eight to ten, making them dance, tumble, and do various tricks with hoops to amuse the drunken audiences. Activists from the Society for the Protection of Animals persecuted the organ grinders for dragging around monkeys and other exotic animals with them.

By the 1860s, the sharmankas and organs of Morits Raush were available in Moscow and St. Petersburg, Nizhny Novgorod, and Warsaw and were especially popular in Tiflis. In the 1880s another Odessite had become a major figure in that market—Konrad Hek. Even in the early twentieth century, when wind organs were being replaced by more modern methods of mechanical reproduction of musical instruments (foremost by the gramophone), the Odessa sharmankas continued to sell well both in the empire and abroad. They were manufactured at the factory of Ivan Viktorovich Nechada, located at 191 Balkovskaya Street, where it borders on Vinogradnaya (today, Isaac Babel Street). Nechada's high-quality and beautifully ornamented sharmankas were used by street musicians for many decades, right up into the 1960s.

Chinese or Russian food can be cooked in New York of Paris, for all it requires is cooks who have mastered the secrets of the cuisine and the right foods and spices, usually imported. But Odessa's musical and poetic folklore, its humor, born in very specific and now mostly lost conditions, have not exported well to other countries, or translated well into other languages, imitation, or re-creation outside of Odessa. In fact, they don't take well to cultivation or professionalization even in modern-day Odessa. But Odessa's folklore and humor served successfully as a base for

No. 30. L. Pasternak
Musikanten

Jewish musicians. Drawing by Leonid Pasternak, early 1890s. Postcard.

the works of Il'f and Petrov, Babel, and today's ironic, wise, and witty humorist Mikhail Zhvanetsky.

The history of Russian photography began in Odessa, where major photography studios opened as early as 1842. Pioneers of photography were an ethnic bouquet: the German F. Haas, Russians A. Khloponin and R. Feodorovets, the Pole I. K. Migursky, the Greek M. Antonopoulos, the Frenchman J. Raoul, the Moldavian V. Dimo, the Ukrainian T. Grigorashenko, and such Jews as M. Likhtenberg and A. Vainshtein. Almost all of them were also painters. Iosif-Karl Migursky founded the Photography Institute in Odessa and published the first textbook on the technology of photography in Russia.

Another legendary figure was Rudolf Feodorovets, acclaimed not only for his photographs but also his talents as hypnotist and spiritualist. The old Odessa photographers won a multitude of prizes and awards in international shows, and in 1891 the International Photography Exhibition took place in Odessa.

Believe it or not, the cinema was invented in Odessa. The inventor's name is Iosif Timchenko, a mechanic from the Imperial New Russia University. In 1893 he created an apparatus that made it possible to project "stroboscopic illusions of interrupted movement" on a screen, and he demonstrated his invention at a learned council of the university. On 11 January 1894—a year before the Lumiére brothers—he published his results. Unfortunately, Timchenko received no financial backing and the first film in Odessa was shown by a representative of the Lumiéres in 1896, in a wooden pavilion constructed in Alexandrovsky Park. Stationary film theaters appeared in the city in 1904. The most famous were Gigant, Beau Monde, Bolshoi Rishelyevsky, Kino-Utochkino, Kometa, Uraniya, and Odeon. The first film studio, Mirograf, belonged to photographer and cameraman M. I. Grosman, who was very active in filming Odessa documentaries in 1907–8. Later he produced feature films, including the popular crime drama *Odessa Catacombs* (1912).

The queen of the Russian silent screen, Vera Kholodnaya (née Levchenko) spent the last part of her life in Odessa, moving there from Moscow. In only three or four years, she made several dozen quality films, working with the best directors and actors, acquiring extraordinary popularity in Russia and abroad. A stage set was being built by a private film studio for *Princess Tarakanova*, starring Kholodnaya. During that time, she was filming in Yalta and giving numerous fundraising concerts for the White Guards. In January 1919, the actress contracted the Spanish flu and died on February 3. Footage of the star's funeral was her last film. This unexpected tragic end gave rise to rumors, gossip, and legends. They say she was poisoned. Or that she had worked in the Bolshevik underground, that she had dealings with such famous expropriators as Grigory Kotovsky and Mishka Yaponchik. These stories became the subject of films like *Slave of Love* and *The Squadron Is Leaving for the West*. The site of the great actress's grave is not known, but a memorial plaque has been placed on the monument of P. I. Chardynin, a director with whom she worked. Of all the films she made, only three have survived, along with the newsreel of her funeral. Yellowed photos recreate the image of the incomparable Vera Levchenko,

Wrappers for Fotograficheskaya caramels, made by the Polyakov Brothers in Odessa.

her mysterious smile addressed, as a poet put it, "to someone who died a century ago."

Unlike the other provincial cities of Russia, Odessa had a large number of periodical publications, from newspapers and magazines to "notes" and "heralds." They were published by the city government, political parties, public organizations, learned societies, educational institutions, religious organizations, and private persons. With topics as varied as politics, literature, business, national issues, medicine, theater, children's topics, women's issues, humor, satire, bibliography, sports, seafaring, charity, and religion, these periodicals addressed those interested in narrow subjects such as the *Journal of Official Data on Brazil* as well as the thousands of subscribers and buyers of *Odesskii vestnik*, *Odesskaya pochta*, or *Odesskii listok*, which published Vlas Doroshevich (the "king of the leaflet" known all over Russia), Ivan Bunin, the just-starting-out Valentin Katayev, and many visiting and local writers. This amounted to a detailed chronicle of Odessa life and events in the country over many decades—from the repertory of the City Theater in Pushkin's time to the abdication of the last Russian tsar, Nicholas II. And while the thematic variety of Odessa's periodicals is impressive, the sheer number is

Above: Vera Kholodnaya and her screen partner, O. I. Runich, in *Forget the Fireplace.*

astonishing: in the period up to early 1920 there were almost 800 periodicals in Russian, Yiddish, Hebrew, Ukrainian, German, Polish, Bulgarian, Serbian, Rumanian, Greek, and French.

As early as the 1840s, local Jewish writers and journalists were published in the newspaper *Odesskii vestnik,* under the aegis of the famous surgeon N. I. Pirogov, head of Odessa's educational region and a patron of Jewish culture. In 1860, through the efforts of the Jewish writer Osip Rabinovich, the first Russian-language Jewish periodical appeared, the weekly *Rassvet (Dawn),* whose aim was "the enlightenment of the people through the exposure of the backwardness of the Jewish masses and bringing them closer to the surrounding population." That same year one of the first periodicals in Hebrew also appeared in Odessa—the weekly *Kha-melits,* founded by A. Tsederbaum, grandfather of Yuli Martov (revolutionary, journalist, and friend of Lenin's).

The development of the Jewish press in Odessa was determined by the Jewish community in a multinational port city and by the socioeconomic and sociopolitical situation in the country. Jewish publications were printed in Hebrew, Yiddish, and Russian, the last having the most publications. The successors to *Rassvet* began publishing weeklies in Russian called *Sion* and *Dyen',* and in the first decades of the twentieth century Odessa newsstands offered local Jewish Russian-language publications like *Sionistskaya rabochaya gazeta (The Zionist Workers' Gazette),* the magazines *Evreiskaya mysl' (Jewish Thought)* and *Russkii Evrei (Russian Jew),* the children's magazine *Kolosiya,* the teenagers' magazine *Molodaya Iudeya,* the professional journal *Evreiskii meditsinskii golos (Jewish Medical Voice),* and the Zionist journal *Kadima.* In 1862, Tsederbaum began publishing the first Russian weekly in Yiddish, *Kol-mevasser,* which printed the writer Medele Mocher Sforim, founder of the professional Jewish theater Avrakham Goldfaden, and writer Moshe Lilienblum. In the early twentieth century the Yiddish newspapers *Gut morgn* and *Sholom aleikhem* were for a mass audience. And even in the turbulent years of the Revolution and Civil War, the literary almanacs *Knesset* and *Erets,* among others, were published. Periodicals in Hebrew debuted in Odessa at the same time as the Russian-language journal *Kha-melits,* and in 1892 the writer and publisher Ravnitsky started the Hebrew almanac *Kha-pardes,* which was the first to publish a poem by the young Chaim Byalik, who was visiting Odessa.

From 1906 until 1919, with a brief hiatus, Doctor of Philosophy I. Klauzner published a literary journal, *Kha-shilloakh,* later banned by the Soviet authorities. Before the Soviet regime came in 1920, *Barkai,* the last Yiddish weekly in Russia, was published in Odessa. Besides periodicals with Zionist or general Jewish interest, Jewish publishers and journalists also published the city-wide newspapers *Odesskaya pochta, Vechernie vedomosti, Odesskii kurier,* and *Odesskie novosti,* one of the most authoritative and

The newspaper *Dyen'* (The Day), the magazines *Evreiskaya Budushch-nost* (Jewish Quotidian) and *Evreiskii Golos* (Jewish Voice).

respectable provincial newspapers in Russia, where Vladimir Jabotinsky made his journalistic debut and which published the stories of Ivan Bunin, Maxim Gorky, Alexander Kuprin, and other visiting and resident writers, both established ones and those just starting out. Odessa owes its literary fame to Jewish writers in particular. The history of Jewish literary Odessa in the nineteenth century involves the names of the poet Eikhenbaum, who wrote in the era of Vorontsov; the playwright Izrail Aksenfeld; the translator Mark Val'tukh, who was the first to translate Pushkin into Italian; and Osip Rabinovich, the first Jewish Russian-language prose writer. At the turn of the century, Odessa had become a major Jewish literary center. Mendele Mocher Sforim wrote in Odessa. He was "the grandfather of Jewish literature" according to his younger contemporary, the great Sholom Aleichem. Like Mocher Sforim, Sholom Aleichem found inspiration for his work in the life of the people, which he returned to them in his books. During 1891–93 Sholom Aleichem lived in Odessa, and his books captured cheerful, sad, bustling, and wise Odessa Jews: craftsmen, teachers, beggars, storekeepers, doctors, and the famous cantor Minkovsky of the Brodsky Synagogue. The great Jewish poet Chaim Byalik lived and worked in Odessa for over two decades. His literary debut took place there, and in 1903 he wrote his epic poem *The Tale of a Pogrom*, based on his visit to Kishinev after a terrible pogrom. Byalik's poem was brilliantly translated into Russian by Jabotinsky, and it became one of the few works of world literature to have a powerful influence on the strengthening of a national identity for Jews. Byalik's call for resistance moved Jewish youths to create self-defense units to protect their fellow Jews from pogroms. Odessa is the birthplace of the poet Sasha Chernyi (Alexander Glikberg), known to all Russians at home and abroad, and the talented prose writer Semyon Yushkevich. The latter wrote in Russian, but all his work is devoted to the lives of Russian Jews. The Jewish writer Sholom Ash stressed that "Yushkevich put his Jewish soul, Jewish heart, Jewish nerves, and Jewish

The magazine *Kadima*.

Advertisement for the film based on Semyon Yushkevich's novel
The Street, 1916.

mind into his work." At the same time, Yushkevich took his place in the pantheon of Russian literature, introducing Jewish themes with talent and without compromise. The specific "Odessa Jew" type, crystallized over the decades, lives on in Yushkevich's books. He died in France, pining for his hometown. In the late nineteeth century, several writers were born in Odessa, including Isaac Babel, Eduard Godelevich Dzubin (Bagritsky), and I. A. Fainzilberg, who took the pseudonym Il'ya Il'f and with his coauthor, Yevgeny Petrov, wrote the well-known satirical novels *The Twelve Chairs* and *The Golden Calf*. Writers Valentin Katayev and Yuri Olesha were also from Odessa.

The Odessa Public Library, the first in the provinces of Russia and the second in the country after the one in the capital of St. Petersburg, was opened in the spring of 1830 when Vorontsov was governor-general. By 1917, the library had over 187,000 titles of books, magazines, and newspapers, including unique editions of Russian and foreign books. The library was funded by the city, exchanges with other libraries, and contributions from private individuals, and for many years was housed in several buildings ill-suited for the purpose until a special building was constructed near Primorsky Boulevard for it and the museum of the Odessa History and Antiquities Society. Eventually the institutions outgrew it. In 1907 the Public Library, with a large reading room, was built (architect F. P. Nesturkh) not far from the university. The benefactor of the library, the Odessa philanthropist Count M. M. Tolstoy, soon purchased the adjoining lot and gave it to the city for the construction of an additional repository, which was done many decades later.

Odessa bade farewell to the nineteenth century with cheer and festivity, celebrating its centenary in 1894 with all the pomp and ceremony such an event requires, publishing a thick volume of the city's history, and building a majestic stock exchange on Pushkinskaya Street. But the new century began with a tragic event. On 14 June 1905, the battleship *Prince Potemkin-Tavrichesky*

Clockwise from page 118: The prison. Drawing by Carlo Bassoli, 1820s; Sonka the Golden Hand; Mishka Yaponchik (Mikhail Vinnitsky), Odessa's most famous bandit, late 1910s.

The building of the original public library and Museum of the History and Antiquities Society. Architect F. Gonsiorovsky. Photograph, 1910s.

of the Black Sea fleet appeared in the port. Its crew scorned its oath and rebelled against the tsar and the legal government of Russia. The sailors of the *Potemkin*, lacking a clear program of action and the support of other ships in the squadron, were defeated. On 18 June the battleship left Odessa for Rumania, where the crew turned themselves in. Those four June days in 1905 were tragic for Odessa: troops were brought into the city and a state of emergency was declared, the port burned, thousands looted and ransacked the warehouses, there were clashes between the citizens and soldiers, there were casualties, the battleship fired twice on the city, and many people abandoned Odessa in a panic.

Twenty years later the great director Sergei Eisenstein made his film *The Battleship Potemkin* in Odessa. Despite its clear-cut ideological bent, it became a film classic. The brilliant scene of the shooting down of citizens on the port steps, which in fact did not happen, was central in the film and the most memorable. Ever since then the stairs have been known as the Potemkin Steps.

The Odessa catacombs are undoubtedly one of the main sights of the city, about which there are many legends and folk beliefs, some of them rooted in truth. Catacombs are artificial tunnels formed in limestone, the main building stone of old Odessa. The limestone stratum around the city is approximately 30 meters below ground and 6–14 meters thick. It formed in remote geological eras, when the Black Sea coast lay on the bottom of the ancient Tethis Ocean, and it is composed of petrified mollusks and shells. The limestone is soft and giving and can easily be sawn into blocks of varying sizes. The stone was quarried even before Odessa was founded. It was used to build the Turkish Eni-Dunya Fortress. Over the hundred and fifty years of quarrying limestone, a multilevel "basement floor" formed beneath Odessa, stretching two thousand kilometers. The catacombs are connected by natural underground spaces, karst caves and grottoes, where remains of extinct animals have been unearthed: saber-toothed tigers, camels, and elephants. The catacombs have not been studied well as yet and still retain their mysteries and puzzles. The legends about an underground city come from the days of the porto-franco: smugglers used the underground passages to avoid the customs posts. In various periods the catacombs served as refuge for criminals. Thieves met to divide their spoils, settle differences, and store their cash, expropriated goods, and valuables. The catacombs were a reliable sanctuary for the persecuted. Both the White Guards and the Soviet partisans hid there, as well as criminals of every type.

One of the streets at Moldavanka was called Glukhaya (Deaf, Quiet), but by the turn of the century it no longer corresponded to the name because of the bordellos that appeared there. In Babel's *Odessa Stories*, there is a casual reference that in the evenings, robbers in Odessa used to gather at Ioska's brothel on Glukhaya Street.

Glukhaya Street was home to the establishment of Iosya Feldman, well known to many Odessa males, and that of his neighbor and rival, Maria Ivanovna. Vice and crime have no age or nationality. In these places, as well as in the houses of Madame Pesi Fruker on Meshchanskaya Street (with a "branch" on Razumovskaya) or of her colleague Madame Yanovskaya near the Privoz Market, one could find a fallen Russian noblewoman, a Ukrainian girl who had come to the big city to work and was seduced by a scoundrel, or a young Jewish girl whose staggering poverty forced her into the brothels of Moldavanka, as described by the Yushkevich in his notorious novel *The Street*, later made into a film.

On Deribasovskaya Street and the adjoining dark alleys, underage prostitutes propositioned passersby, whose pockets were picked by Odessa's Oliver Twists—boys who were trained at the "thieves school" of the elderly crime authority Ruvim Freidenberg. The police were also interested in the venerable thief and con man Moisey Zilberman, known as Moishe Oks, who could deceive a famous actress or brave general as easily as unwary locals or the simple and trusting hicks visiting Odessa.

But the acknowledged king of Odessa's thieves was Mikhail Vinnitsky, also known as Mishka Yaponchik. Living in the criminal world from a young age and having served time in prison, he developed his own concept of justice. An extraordinary and ambitious man, he created in 1918 a kind of criminal corporation and became the Robin Hood of Odessa. In any case, it was Yaponchik's men who protected Odessa from the Jewish pogroms that were breaking out all over Ukraine. His authority, power, and influence were enormous. He was captured and executed in the early years of Soviet rule.

Sonka Golden Hand was one of the most vivid romantic figures of the Odessa criminal world. The many romantic legends about her lack basis in reality. In historical literature she usually figures under the surname Bluvshtein, but that is merely the name of one of her many husbands, Moishe Bluvshtein, who was tried

with her in 1880 in the same case. The legends make her younger, claiming that she was born in 1869. That is silly in view of the fact that she was first tried in the courts in 1872: it is unlikely that three-year-olds were accused of serious crimes.

In fact Sonka was a middle-class woman from Warsaw, née Solomoniak in 1846. She became Golden Hand in the 1860s, when she worked as a con artist and thief on the newfangled railroads. Charming and bold to the point of obnoxiousness,

Kindergarten on the lower terrace of Nikolaevsky (Primorsky) Boulevard. Postcard, 1910s.

Sonka easily seduced unwary travelers, who paid later with their suitcases and bags. The work was dangerous but profitable: one case is known of her making 213,000 rubles on one trip. Later, Sonka formed a powerful crime syndicate that worked the large Russian fairs, primarily the one in Nishny Novgorod. They were typical touring criminals. The gang was almost completely Jewish, which led to a series of prejudiced accounts, including those published in the last century in *Evreiskie rechi* by anti-Semites. This does not justify the criminal activity of Sonka and her gang. Odessa was one of the main bases for the syndicate. The thieving prima donna rested there after her labors, living off her ill-gotten gains. Their cash holdings were kept in Odessa and sometimes the entire company of Sonka's husbands gathered there. She was arrested in Odessa on 27 August 1879. Exiled to Siberia, she escaped, was recaptured, and eventually ended up on Sakhalin Island, where Chekhov saw her.

Born during the reign of Catherine the Great, Odessa paid the empress her due. In 1898 on a small square near Primorsky Boulevard and the statue of the Duc de Richelieu, a monument to the Empress was erected (architect Yu. Dmitrenko, sculptor B. Edwards). This is a full-size bronze statue of Catherine on a tall cylindrical pedestal, and around it are bronze statues of Prince Potemkin-Tavrichesky, Admiral de Ribas, De Voland, and Count Platon Zubov, in whose honor one of the piers of the port is called Platonovsky. After the Revolution of February 1917, which put an end to the Russian Empire, the statue was covered with canvas so that there would not be a symbol of the former rule in the middle of town. But no one damaged it, and if not for the October Bolshevik Revolution that year, it would have stood in its original place, as a work of art and embodiment of Odessa's historical memory. However, once the Bolsheviks took over, the new city authorities sent sailors to the square on May 1, 1920, they threw ropes over the statues and used horses to drag it from the pedestal.

Odessa was born at the sunset of the scintillating eighteenth century, and like a bird shot on the wing, was wounded by the tragic events of the twentieth century. It was a city of geniuses and madmen, talented administrators and wise businessmen, generous philanthropists and merry adventures, marvelous women and mocking poets.

A lovely myth. A lovely city.

Scene from *The Battleship Potemkin*. Courtesy of Moscow Film Museum.

Лѣстница при

L'escalier

The steps on Nikolayevsky (Primorsky) Boulevard. Architect, F. Boffo, 1842. Postcard, 1900s.

Monument to Catherine II the Great, 1898. Architect Yu.
Dmitrenko; sculptor B. Edwards. Postcard, 1900s.

Одесса. Памятникъ Екатерины II.
Odessa. Monument Catherine II.

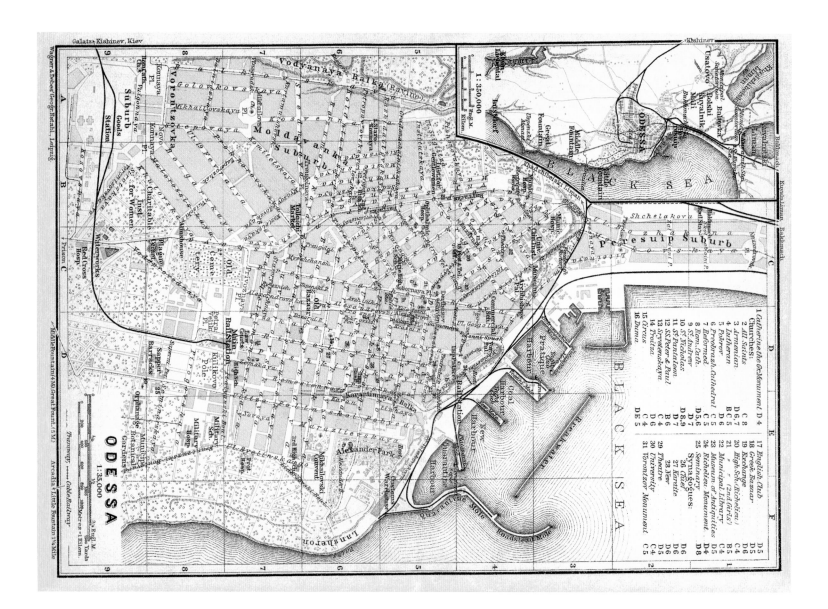

Bibliography

Abramovitsh, S. Y. *Tales of Mendele the Book Peddler.* Edited by Dan Miron and Ken Frieden. New York: Schocken Books, 1996.

Aleichem, Sholom. *The Adventures of Menahem-Mendl.* Translated by Tamara Kahana. New York: Putnam, 1969.

Alexandrov, Rostislav. *Progulki po literaturnoi Odesse.* Odessa: Vest', 1993.

———. *S Ranyogo Vremeni.* Odessa: Optimum, 2002.

Ascherson, Neal. *Black Sea.* New York: Hill and Wang, 1995.

Atlas, Dorothea. *Staraia Odessa, ee druz'ia i nedrugi.* Odessa: Lasmi, 1992.

Babel, Isaac. *The Complete Works of Isaac Babel.* Edited by Nathalie Babel. Translated with notes by Peter Constantine. New York: W. W. Norton and Company, 2002.

———. *The Lonely Years, 1925–1939.* Translated by Andrew MacAndrew and Max Hayward. Edited with an introduction by Nathalie Babel. New York: David R. Godine, 1964.

Berman, V. *Odessa.* Moscow, 1990.

Bernshtein, Simon. *Odessa: Istoricheskii i torgovo-ekonomicheskii ocherk Odessy v sviazi s Novorossiiskim kraem.* Odessa: L. Nitshe, 1881.

Briker, Boris. "The Underworld of Benya Krik and I. Babel's *Odessa Stories.*" *Canadian Slovonic Papers/ Revue Canadienne des Slavistes* 36, nos. 1–2 (1994): 115–34.

Brown, Clarence, ed. *The Portable Twentieth-Century Russian Reader.* New York: Penguin Books, 1985.

Brun, F. *Sud'by mestnosti, zanimaemoi Odesoiu.* Odessa, 1865.

Cheremisinov, V. M. *Napadenie anglo-frantsuzskogo flota na Odessu v 1854.* Odessa, 1904.

———. *Odessa v istorii russkikh voin: k 50–letiiu Krymskoi voiny.* Odessa, 1904.

Clark, Katerina, and Michael Holmquist. *Mikhail Bakhtin.* Cambridge: Harvard University Press, 1984.

Dallin, Alexander. *Odessa, 1941–1944: A Case Study of Soviet Territory under Foreign Rule.* Iasi, Romania: Center for Romanian Studies, 1998.

Одесса. Городская Публичная Библіотека.
Odessa. Biblioteque de ville.

Dawidowicz, Lucy S. *The Golden Tradition: Jewish Life and Thought in Eastern Europe.* Syracuse: Syracuse University Press, 1996.

De-Volant, General François. *The Essay of My Service in Russia, 1787–1811.* Odessa: Odessa Trading Seaport, 1999.

Dobrovolskyi, Andrei, Oleg Gubar, and Andrei Krasnozhon. "Borisfen-Khadzhubei-Odessa." *Vyshaya antropologichnaya Shkola,* 2002.

Friedberg, Maurice. *How Things Were Done in Odessa: Cultural and Intellectual Pursuits in a Soviet City.* Boulder: Westview Press, 1991.

Frieden, Ken. *Classic Yiddish Fiction: Abramovitsh, Sholom Aleichem, and Peretz.* Albany: State University of New York Press, 1995.

Green, Michael, and Jerome Katsell, eds. and trans. *Yury Olesha: The Complete Plays.* Ann Arbor: Ardis Publishers, 1983.

Gubar, Oleg. *100 voprosov iz Odessy.* Odessa: Polinom, 1994.

———. *Puskin, teatr, Odessa.* Odessa: Kinotsentr, 1993.

———. *Vsmatrivaias' v litsa: K 155-letiiu fotografii v Odesse.* Odessa, 1998.

Gubar, O., E. Golubovskyi, and P. Alexandrov. *Odessa: Yearly Almanach.* Odessa: S. F. Yakovlev, 2002.

Hausmann, Guido. *Universität und städtische Gesellschaft in Odessa, 1865–1917.* Stuttgart: Franz Steiner Verlag, 1998.

Одесса   Николаевскій бульваръ.

Herlihy, Patricia. *Odessa: A History, 1794–1914.* Cambridge: Harvard University Press, 1986.

———. "Commerce and Architecture in Odessa and Late Imperial Russia." In *Commerce in Russian Urban Culture, 1861–1914.* Edited by William Craft Brumfield, Boris V. Anan'ich, and Yuri A. Petrov, pp. 180–94. Washington, D.C., and Baltimore: Johns Hopkins University Press, 2001.

Il'f, Il'ya, and Evgeny Petrov. *The Golden Calf.* Translated by John H. C. Richardson. New York: Random House, 1962.

Istoricheshyi-Kraevedetshkoy I Literaturnyi-Khudozhostvennoy Almanach (quarterly journal).

Jabotinsky, Vladimir. "Memoirs by My Typewriter." In *The Golden Tradition*, edited by Lucy S. Dawidowicz. Syracuse: Syracuse University Press, 1996.

Kamennyi, Aleksandr. *Odessa: Who Is Who (1794–1994).* Odessa: OKFA, 1999.

Katz, Shmuel. *Lone Wolf: A Biography of Vladimir (Ze'ev) Jabotinsky,* vol. 1. New York: Barricade Books, 1996.

Koschmal, Walter, ed. *Odessa: Kapitel aus der Kulturgeschichte.* Regensburg: Michael Lassleben, 1998.

Kotler, Yigal. *Ocherki po istorii evreev Odessy.* Jerusalem: Noy, 1996.

Kozak, Anatolii F. *Odessa zdes' bol'she ne zhivet.* Samara: Tarbut, 1997.

Kuprin, A. *Sasha.* Translated by Douglas Ashby. London: S. Paul and Co., 1920

Luker, Nicholas. *Alexander Kuprin.* Boston: Twayne Publishers, 1987.

Lvov, Arkady. *The Courtyard*. New York: Doubleday, 1989.

Maistrovoy, Ya, ed. *Ulitsy Odessy: Spravochnik po toponomii staroi chasti goroda*. Kursk: A. P. Kursk, 1998.

Markevich, A. *Gorod Kachibei ili Gadzhibei-predshestvennik goroda Odessy*. Odessa, 1894.

Mikhnevich, Iosif. *Biografiia gertsoga de Rishel'e*. Odessa, 1849.

Musées de Marseille. *La mémoire d'Odessa*. Paris: Hatier, 1989.

Nadler, V. K. *Odessa v pervye epokhi ee sushchestvovaniia*. Odessa, 1893.

Odessa: Ocherk istorii goroda-geroia k 150–letiiu so dnia osnovaniia. Odessa, 1947.

Odessa, 1794–1894. Izdanie gorodskogo obshchestvennogo upravleniia k stoletiiu goroda

Olesha, Yuri. *No Day Without a Line*. Ann Arbor: Ardis Publishers, 1979.

———. *Love and Other Stories*. Translated by Robert Payne. New York: Washington Square Press, 1967.

Orbach, Alexander. *New Voices of Russian Jewry: A Study of the Russian-Jewish Press of Odessa in the Era of the Great Reforms, 1860–1871*. Leiden: E. J. Brill, 1980.

Orlov, A. *Istoricheskii ocherk Odessy s 1794 po 1803*. Odessa, 1885.

Paustovsky, Konstantin. *Story of a Life*. 5 vols. Translated by Manya Harari and Michael Duncan. London: Harvill Press; New York: Pantheon, 1965–69.

Penter, Tanja. *Odessa 1917: Revolution an der Peripherie*. Köln: Böhlau Verlag, 2000.

Peppard, Victor. *The Poetics of Yury Olesha*. Gainesville: University of Florida Press, 1989.

Poizner, M. B. *Iz podsmotrennogo i podshlushannogo v Odesse*. Odessa: LIA Odessey, 1997.

Polishtshuk, Mikhail. *Evreiy Odessy i Novorosii* (Social-political history of the Jews in Odessa and other towns in Novorossia, 1881–1904). Moscow: Mosty Kultury, 2001.

———. *Moscow and Jerusalem*. Moscow: Mosty Kultury, 2001.

Reeder, Roberta. *Anna Akhmatova: Poet and Prophet*. New York; Picador, 1995.

Reid, Anna. *Borderland: A Journey Through the History of Ukraine*. London: Weidenfeld and Nicolson, 1997.

Ribas, Aleksandr de. *Staraia Odessa: Istoricheskie ocherki, vospominaniia*. Odessa, 1913. Facsimile reprint, Moscow: Dimoff and Co., 1995.

Ribas, Michele de. *Saggio sulla Città di Odessa*. Edited by Giovanna Moracci. Genoa: Cassa di Risparmio di Genova e Imperia, 1988.

Rothstein, Robert A. "How It Was Sung in Odessa: At the Intersection of Russian and Yiddish Folk Culture." *Slavic Review* 60, no. 4 (Winter 2001): 781–801.

Salys, Rimgaila, ed. *Olesha's Envy: A Critical Companion*. Evanston, Ill.: Northwestern University Press, 1999.

Sarkissian, Konstantin, and Mikhail Stavnitser. *Ulitsy raskazyvaiut*. Odessa: Mayak, 1968.

Schneiderman, Jeremiah. *Sergei Zubatov and Revolutionary Marxism: The Struggle for the Working Class in Tsarist Russia*. Ithaca: Cornell University Press, 1976.

Shrayer, Maxim. *Russian Poet/Soviet Jew: The Legacy of Eduard Bagritskii.* Lanham, Md.: Rowman and Littlefield, 2000.

Skal'kovskii, Apollon. *Admiral de Ribas i zavoevanie Khadzhibeia, 1764–1797.* Odessa, 1889.

———. *Khronologiskoe obozrenie istorii Novorossiiskogo kraia, 1730–1823.* Part One: 1730–1796, Odessa, 1836. Part Two: 1796–1823, Odessa, 1838.

———. *Pervoe tridtsatiletie istorii goroda Odessy, 1793–1823.* Odessa, 1837.

Smol'ianinov, K. *Istoriia Odessy.* Odessa, 1853.

Solodova, Vera, and Larissa Fabrika. *Odessa v proizvedeniakh grafiki XIX veka.* Odessa: Odessa State Scientific Library, 1995.

Stanislawski, Michael. *Zionism and the Fin de Siècle: Cosmopolitanism and Nationalism from Nordau to Jabotinsky.* Berkeley: University of California Press, 2001.

Starr, S. Frederick. *Red and Hot: The Fate of Jazz in the Soviet Union, 1917–1980.* New York: Oxford University Press, 1983.

Stites, Richard. *Russian Popular Culture: Entertainment and Society since 1900.* Cambridge: Cambridge University Press, 1992.

Sylvester, Roshanna P. "Crime, Masquerade, and Anxiety: The Public Creation of Middle Class Identity in Pre-Revolutionary Odessa, 1912–1916." Ph.D. dissertation, Yale University, 1998.

Taruskin, Richard. *Defining Russia Musically: Historical and Hermaneutical Essays.* Princeton: Princeton University Press, 1997.

Teplish, Alexander. *Odessa-Zhemchuzhina u moria: Pesni i zabytye tantseval'nye melodii.* Odessa: Yuzhnaya Initsiativa, 1998.

Timofeenko, V. I. *Odessa: Arkhitekturo-istoricheskii ocherk.* Kiev: Budivelnik, 1983.

Vsia Odessa: Antologia-Slovar'. Moscow: Dimoff and Co., 1997.

Weinberg, Robert. *The Revolution of 1905 in Odessa: Blood on the Steps.* Bloomington: Indiana University Press, 1993.

———. *Stalin's Forgotten Zion: Birobizhan and the Making of a Soviet Jewish Homeland, An Illustrated History, 1928–1996.* Berkeley: University of California Press, 1998.

Weiner, Miriam. *Jewish Roots in Ukraine and Moldova: Pages from the Past and Archival Inventories.* New York: YIVO, 1999.

Yeykelis, Igor. "Odessa 1914–1922: The Resurgence of Local Social and Cultural Values During the Times of Upheaval." Ph.D. dissertation, Melbourne University, 1997.

Zipperstein, Steven J. *The Jews of Odessa: A Cultural History, 1794–1881.* Stanford: Stanford University Press, 1985.

Illustration Credits

The authors are very grateful to those who were generous in loaning postcards and photographs for this book, illustrations are used courtesy of the following (listed alphabetically by owner):

Oleg Gubar Collection

pages xxii, 48, 96, 108

Nicolas V. Iljine Collection

pages ii (bottom), iii, iv, v (bottom), vi, vii, viii, ix, x, xi, xii, xiii, xiv, xv, xvi, xvii, xviii, xxx, xxxviii, xxxix, xl, xli, xlii, xliii, xliv, xlvi, xlvii, 12, 13, 14, 15, 18, 21, 22, 25, 26, 29, 30, 33, 40, 41, 42, 43, 44, 46, 47, 50, 51, 53 (right), 57, 60, 66, 70, 77, 78, 79, 85, 86, 89 (top), 90, 97, 110, 121, 124, 125, 126, 127, 130, 131, 132, 133, 134, 135

Bel Kaufman

pages xlviii, li, liv

Pavel Khoroshilov Collection

pages xxiv, xxv

Moscow Film Museum

pages xxxii, xxxv, 122

National Library of Russia

pages ii (top), v (top), xxi, xxvi, xxvii, xxviii, xlv, 2, 3, 5, 6, 9, 10, 56 (bottom right), 62, 80, 81, 82, 83, 84, 98, 99, 100, 104, 105, 107, 109, 115, 116, 117, 120

OGNB (Odessa Scientific Library)

pages 53, 57

Odessa State Historical Regional Studies Museum

page 52

Private collection

pages xxxvi, 73

M. B. Poizner Collection

pages xxiii, 89, 101, 112, 121

YIVO Institute for Jewish Research, New York

pages 69 (right), 71 (right), 74, 89 (bottom), 92 (bottom right)

Index

Contributors

NICOLAS V. ILJINE, European representative of the Solomon R. Guggenheim Foundation, has more than thirty years' experience dealing in cultural exchange with Russia.

BEL KAUFMAN is the grandaughter of Sholem Aleichem and herself an author of renown. Her novel *Up the Down Staircase* has been translated into sixteen languages and was made into a major motion picture in 1967.

PATRICIA HERLIHY is research professor at the Watson Institute for International Studies at Brown University and professor emeritus of history, Brown University. She is the author of *Odessa: A History, 1774–1914*, which was issued in English and Ukrainian.

OLEG GUBAR, a sixth-generation Odessite, attended middle school No. 92, served in the Soviet army, studied at the Naval Engineering Institute, and graduated from I. I. Mechnikov Odessa State University. He has published a dozen books on a variety of subjects and has won a number of Russia's literary prizes.

ALEXANDER ROZENBOIM, an engineer, studied at the Construction Institute, Odessa, and first encountered historical Odessa as part of a research project on the history of the city's plumbing, in collaboration with Professor Grigory Bass and later with Yevgeny Golubovsky. Under the pseudonym of Rostislav Alexandrov, he has published seven books on Odessa's history and produced dozens of television programs.

ANTONINA W. BOUIS has translated numerous works, including *St. Petersburg: A Cultural History* by Solomon Volkov and *Dust and Ashes* by Anatoli Rybakov.

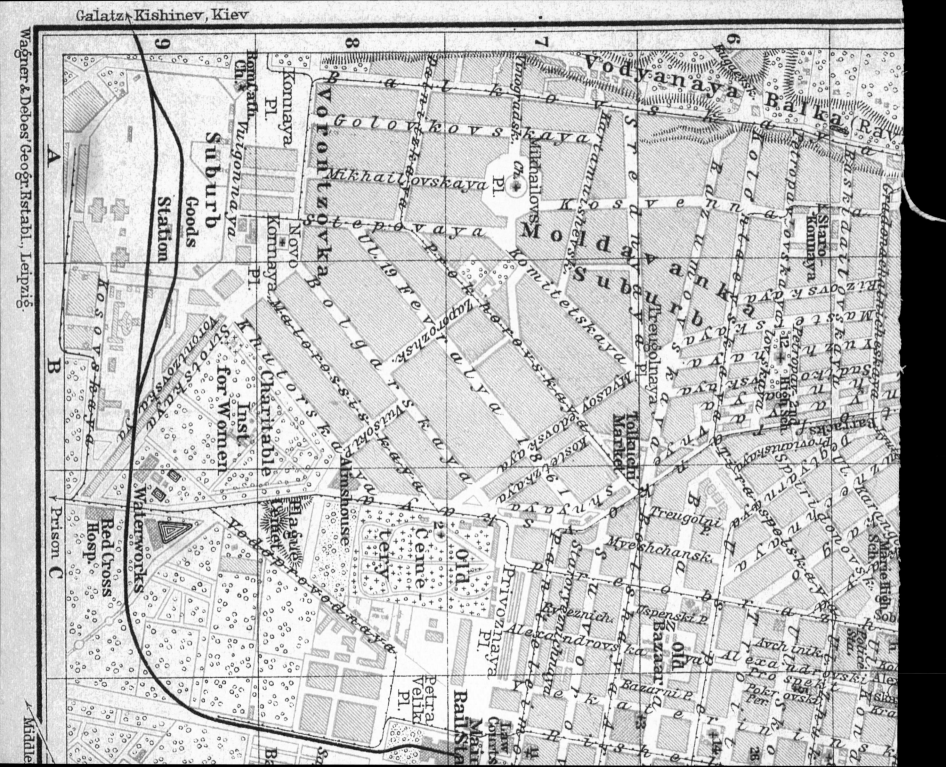